Open Road to Faraway

Also by Andrew S Winton

Twenty Most Favourite Songs of Burns
ISBN 0 85683 1751
Shepheard-Walwyn, London 1998

Open Road
to Faraway

Escapes from Nazi POW Camps
1941-1945

Andrew S Winton

Cualann Press

ISBN 0 9535036 5 8

First Edition September 2001

British Library Cataloguing in Publication Data. A catalogue record of this book is available at the British Library.

Printed by Bell & Bain, Glasgow

Published by:
Cualann Press, 6 Corpach Drive, Dunfermline, KY12 7XG, Scotland
Email: cualann@btinternet.com
Website: http://users.ouvip.com/cualann/

Dedication

This book is dedicated to the memory of my grandson Ronnie, who at twelve years of age, stepped quietly on to the Open Road to Faraway.

It is also dedicated to my other five grandchildren
Andrew and Murray
Michael
Seán and Sarah

And He that wisna oor Kith an'Kin,
But a Prince o' the Far Awa',
Gaithered the weans in His airms,
An' blessed them ane an' a'.

Acknowledgements

I am greatly indebted to Kathleen, my wife, and all other members of my family, for their encouragement and help in the production of my memoirs. A special thanks is due to Mrs Janine Smillie who volunteered to type my script.

Biographical Note

Andrew Winton, from the small village of Woolfords near Lanark, was a student at the Edinburgh College of Art before enlisting with the RAF soon after the outbreak of the Second World War. Shot down over Germany on 30th September 1941, he spent the next four years attempting to escape back home from Nazi Prisoner of War Camps to his beloved Scottish moors.

Each escape was, however, short-lived. Following one escape of seventeen days, he experienced the horrors of Buchenwald Concentration Camp – the worst few days of his life. The final stage of the war was fraught with hazards in the chaos that followed the German retreat. Andrew and his comrades were eventually handed over to the Americans by the Russians at the River Elbe.

After the war, Andrew gave evidence of his wartime treatment at the Nuremberg Trials where he was also called upon to confirm reports about his captors. He resumed his studies at the Edinburgh College of Art and later taught art in a number of Edinburgh schools before becoming assistant rector at Trinity Academy.

Andrew's love of Burns' poetry frequently sustained him in captivity. His lifelong ambition to re-pay his debt to the national bard was realised when his remarkable book, *Twenty Most Favourite Songs of Burns* in his own calligraphic script and decorated with flowers and grasses loved by Burns, was published three years ago.

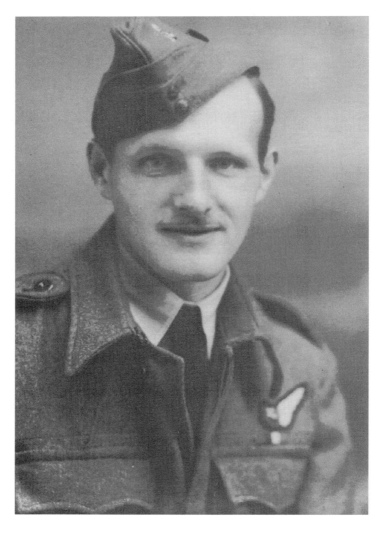

Warrant Officer A S Winton, Royal Air Force Volunteer Reserve

Contents

Illustrations

Foreword

What you are about to read are memories. They are of a man who, quite literally, fell into a nightmare world. In many ways, it is also a story about the power of memory itself, both as a precious refuge in the face of unimaginable horror and as an involuntary recorder and reminder of that same reality.

In September 1941, Andrew Winton baled out of his RAF bomber into a continent of Europe under the control of Nazi Germany. He found himself in a strange, paradoxical world where social order and the basic rule and process of law were drowning in a rising tide of totalitarian violence and brutality. As a British prisoner of war, he experienced and describes the contradictions, harshness and absurdities that such a life entailed – escape committees, Red Cross parcels, occasional beatings from guards and the crushing boredom. He evokes a society striving to maintain a measure of cohesion in the face of captors who, as the war progressed were, ironically, trying to do the same. As the Allies advanced and their bombing increased, so shortages of food and the long German retreat westwards levelled the barriers between captives and captors. Life over the wire was even more extreme. The author's experiences 'on the run', recalled with the clarity of an artist's memory, cross over into the surreal as he is trapped between the retreating Germans and the advancing Red Army. He describes a disintegrating world where people are adrift and are ready to cling to whatever vestige of decency, family, love or beauty they can find. Again and again, memory provides Andrew Winton and the people he comes across with their only hope in a disintegrating world.

For the author, it is the memory of his home in Lanarkshire, and of the Scottish landscape in particular, that sustained him. Just as the horrors he witnessed were seared into his memory, so he carried the imprint of moorland and loch, and the words of Robert Burns. Like many before him caught up in the chaos of war, these are the things that gave him strength and hope and spurred him to escape the confinement of the prisoner. It wasn't hatred for the enemy or love of 'King and Country' that made him dream and plan of escape; it was the power of memory.

In the early part of his story, Andrew Winton describes the last summer of peace in Scotland. He is on his uncle's farm near Cleish in Kinross-shire. As they look out over ripening fields, his uncle says, 'A pity you didn't have a sheet of paper and paints with you, Andy. Isn't that a great picture'? Andrew replies 'I'll store it in my memory and send it on to you when I have it finished'.

I don't know if he ever finished that picture but over the next six years his memory stored many such pictures, for better or for worse.

Allan L Carswell
Curator
National War Museum of Scotland

Preface

The first month back home after my time in Germany was a quiet spell, just as the RAF medical officers who had examined me had ordered. It was obvious that something was wrong with me, but I was so desperate to be back and out on the moor, that I said nothing about the blackouts that were troubling me. Nevertheless I resolved to return to Art College and finish my course, and to this end I decided to spend a day in Edinburgh.

The first person I met at the College was Davie Ballingal, the under-janitor. Putting down his broom he came over and took my hands.

'It's you, Andy, man. It's good to see you again!'

'And you too, Davie.'

'Come away in; it's tea break – and we'll meet the others – there've been a few changes.'

While drinking tea, I mentioned that I would have to see the Principal. He was away, 'returning tomorrow', I was informed and so I decided to walk around for a while and return the next day. Curiosity pointed my feet in the direction of the textile room. I opened the door and had taken three steps into the room before I saw a tutor, Betty Forbes, standing, her back to the window, with six or seven female students around her. Betty put down her cigarette and said, 'It's Andy, isn't it?' I nodded and began to reverse. The green mist that always preceded a blackout came down, and before I reached the door, I was on my knees.

I opened my eyes to find that I was lying on a white sheet, a network of curtain rails with closed curtains around, and a blue and white dressed nurse standing looking at me. I lay thinking for a minute. If there was something wrong with me I might not be allowed to proceed to teacher training. What now? I moved my hands and made to rise and spoke quietly.

'If you bring me my clothes, I'll just go.'

A very firm hand held me down.

'You have to lie quietly. Someone is coming to see you.'

A young male doctor came in.

'It's Andy, isn't it?'

I nodded.

'I'm here to find out what happened. I'll pass on everything to a colleague. We've already got information from the Art College; we'll check on that later. You've just come back from the RAF?'

I nodded again. There was a long pause, and then he added softly, 'When we stripped you when you came in, we saw the marks all over your body. How did that happen?'

I considered for a minute. I decided to tell all.

'If you don't mind,' he said, 'I'll record this.'

Twenty minutes or so later, an elderly doctor came in. The doctors listened through until the end, asking questions every now and then. They talked quietly for a while at the end of the bed.

'Now tell us what happened in Art College this morning.'

'I had a blackout'.

I considered for a moment, then thought: if I don't tell, they won't know what to treat. And so I told them about Berlin: the destruction and wrecking of property and population; the raping and murder of females of all ages; of hunger and fear and misery and the continual desire for food. And I told them about a house into which I had wandered. The mother hanging by a pulley rope, naked and bleeding, her clothes ripped in a search for jewellery … and her throat cut. The eldest daughter also stripped and raped and a baby with its head bashed lying across the mother's mouth to suffocate her … the second girl lying in a corner also raped and dead, and the third child, almost unrecognisable, cut and bleeding where a knife had traced the beginning-to-grow bosoms and nipples gouged out with a sharp knife point. I stopped.

'That's what I saw when I looked at the class. I'm going to be working in that room. When will my head clear?'

A short conference followed.

'We'd like to keep you here for observation for a day or two. Meanwhile, nurse will get all details and something to drink.'

I was left to ponder. The Art College course was probably the best thing for me. The blackouts would gradually wane, I was to keep in touch once a fortnight and to avoid occasions of stress.

And so it was. Time was the big healing factor. Three years later I was almost clear of blackouts, had passed all exams and was accepted as an art teacher in Edinburgh schools.

Completely immersed in my teaching, time passed quickly. I began to read as many biographies as I could find on the life of Burns and sang and recited his works on fishing trips over the moor. I met an Irish lady, a nurse, and fell in love. This was, without doubt, a major factor in my recovery. We married and had three children: a boy, then a girl followed by another boy. Following many years' work I published a book in calligraphic script of some of the songs of Robert Burns and then the grandchildren ordered me to write my 'history'. And so began *Open Road to Faraway*, with the fond hope that they, and their peers, would read and realise that there was no glamour in the field of war.

Andrew Sneddon Winton

Chapter 1

Early Days

High on the hill, north of the village of Woolfords, was the figure of a boy. One moment seen, then he disappeared, then back into view higher up. There he stood on a flat stone and gazed all around. Away to the south, clear against a pale blue sky, was Tinto Hill. Following the horizon to the east came the tail end of the Pentland Hills. Westward there was a flatter horizon, a few trees showing and a church steeple at Forth. Slowly the gaze came back to Tinto. Somewhere at the bottom, in the Clyde Valley, was the town of Lanark. The thought of the town, although he had never been there, took the boy's mind back to William Wallace. He would somehow send a message to say that the moor was empty – no English horsemen killing sheep. If he could reach the Skinny Wood Hill he'd be able to see more and maybe Wallace would make him an outrider!

Dropping down into the rushes at the burnside, he wriggled quickly along to the high wood. On the hilltop was a sheep shelter; he slipped into it and moved round to one side. There he took a stone from the dyke and looked long and hard at the fields below. Half a mile away five men and a horse were working at the hay. Still no English soldiers, and then into the shelter came Glen, tail wagging, and further down the hill, the shepherd, John Lambie, appeared. The stone was put back into the hole and wedged with a sharpened stick. The game was over. The playground came back to normal.

'Hullo, John, it's a nice day.'

'O aye, Andrew, if it stays like this we'll maybe clip tomorrow. You can come along and help Davie drive.'

'I'll ask my mother.'

We wandered down the hill, picking up odd bits of wool.

'School on Monday?' John asked. I nodded: the very mention of Auchengray sent a shiver down my back.

'You'll be all right there. Auld JMC will see that you don't get into mischief.'

There it was again: that quiet threat of the Headmaster. Uncle Jim had said, 'He'll sort you out: he's got a big new belt for you lot after the holiday,' and Mother had said, 'Don't you listen to him, he's got nothing of the sort.'

As John and Glen turned away, John said, 'Here's a bag of wool for your Mother. Tell her you were helping me.'

'Thanks, John, maybe she'll let me go tomorrow; bye.'

I ran all the way home. Father met me at the door.

'Where have you been? Your Mother's worried sick.'

'I was up the field.'

Mother came in, clearly relieved at my return as I would sometimes 'run away' up to the moor.

'Oh, you got some wool for me? That's nice' she said, fingering the wool thoughtfully.

I was with Miss Hodge for my first two years of school and everything was easy. I started to read and write and count and liked my work. I could recite my first book from beginning to end. Things were different in my third year and I struggled to please the 'Maister' until Uncle Jim told me that if I learned to recite Rabbie Burns' poems or sing his songs, I would get on fine. When Mrs Lindsay, the school cleaner, told the Maister that I was to recite in the local hall at a Burns' Supper, he wrote to Mother for permission to coach me for five minutes at the end of each day. The answer was 'Yes' and I started my extra lesson.

The school emptied and the Maister came in with a cup of tea.

'So you're going to recite, Andrew?'

'Yes, sir.'

'And what are you starting off with?'

'*To a Mouse*, Sir, by Robert Burns.'

'Let's hear it.'

I rattled off the first verse in one breath, standing straight and looking out at an imaginary audience.

He stopped me. 'No, no, Andrew. We'll need to think about this. Here was Rabbie at the plough and a wee mouse jumps out. He picks it up and speaks to it. Do you think he'd be standing like a fence pole? Oh no. He was speaking to a wee mouse, half the size of his thumb and gently stroking it with his other hand. Now, another thing. I want you to take a breath between each word, but we'll do that tomorrow.'

'Thank you, sir,' and I was away.

All the way home I kept repeating the poem, one word at a time and taking a breath after each word. The next night he produced a little ball of grey wool and said the words of the poem to me. He was now so different to the schoolteacher that I knew. I tried to copy him; he became Rabbie Burns. None of the other children would ever have seen him like this. Word for word, line after line, verse after verse, and I was speaking to a wee field mouse.

The concert was a great success. Willie Campbell brought in his pet mouse and I held it in my hand. A woman in the front row screamed when she saw it and had to be given a glass of water. Then I said my poem to complete silence. When I finished, the audience clapped. Big

Jock Dunlop shouted, 'Say it again', but the MC explained that I would recite another one, *To a Daisy,* later.

I learned quite a few poems before I left Auchengray and lost the initial terror I had for schools. When I went to Lanark to the Grammar School I met many very fine teachers, especially the art staff who encouraged me to go on to the College of Art in Edinburgh, and John Mathieson, Deputy Rector and Scottish scholar, who dropped my first essay on to my desk with the dry remark, 'Andrew Sneddon Winton. You'll have to do better than that if you're to follow your ancestor.'

Chapter 2

Grandad

Grandad taught me much about the world.

As we set out to the carrot and turnip field one morning, I called, 'Grandad!' He stopped and looked at me.

'What are we going to discuss the day?'

I walked on for a few steps, then asked, 'When you were a wee laddie, like me, did your Grandad teach you all the things you tell me?'

'Oh no. There's some things you are shown what to do, but there's other things you learn for yourself just by using your eyes and ears. Here, sit ower here.'

I moved from the carrots to where he sat.

'Listen, that lark's sang has changed.'

Down out of the sky came a lark, fluttering its wings: down, down to a threshie bush, then up again for three or four feet, all the time singing hard notes, and down again to another bush.

'Is it hurt, Grandad?'

'Wheest – just watch.'

Out of the second bush came a long, sinewy brown body: a small
dark head with black shining eyes and a white
stripe on the underside. It too was singing:
cheerie cheetie, chi chi chee, repeating and
swaying. Down came the lark again, wings
fluttering and checking and then up and over
to another bush. Again the body appeared.

'It's trying to hypnotise the lark,'
whispered Grandad. Twice more the act went
on, each time going further away from where
it started. Soon, the lark rose higher and
changed its song.

'Thank goodness it didn't catch it,' I
said. Grandad held me down beside him.

'Look at the gate – it's not finished
yet.'

I looked. On the hinge post was a lovely barn owl almost the
same colour as the post, its round staring eyes looking down on to the
field. Suddenly, it dropped sideways, came round in a circle and with
razor sharp claws at full stretch, went straight into the threshes. A flap of
wings and it rose. Hanging from one foot was the bent, dead body of the
weasel.

'It's away to the mill ring. It must have young ones. And noo,
come down here where we saw it starting. Watch your feet now!'

Slowly we went forward and then I saw it. A lovely wee nest set
into a bank of thick grass. From it rose a little brown lark to sit on top of
the bank and chirp at us for disturbing it. And there in the nest were four
little eggs.

'We'll keep an eye on it,' said Grandad and we moved away.

The watcher in the sky started his song again and the little hen
hopped back to keep her eggs warm.

'Now we'll go down to the burnside and I'll show you how to use a scythe. Do you see the difference between one form of learning and another? The world goes on like that all the time. Folks are just the same as the birds and animals. You never know what to expect. But thinning carrots and cutting grass is a job that's always the same.'

Down at the burn, Grandad's scythe was leaning against a fence post. When he picked it up it seemed to fit him, just like a waistcoat or a fine jacket. He showed me how to sharpen the blade; how to set the blade; how to lay it to the grass and then the gentle sweep to cut and leave the surface flat and smooth.

'You're too young to start,' he said, 'You would need a light one like your big cousin, Jock. He'll be good when he does a bit every day. He's got the job of dressing the tennis courts in Kinross and he pleases the members.'

I said nothing, but deep inside I determined I'd be as good as Jock some day.

Chapter 3

War

For a first time run, the road from Queensferry to Dunfermline was interesting. Wanting to go to Cleish because I had been told that my grandparents had been married there, I took the Townhill road.

Keeping the Cleish Hills and the Dumblow beacon light on my left, I finally reached the village. As it was late afternoon and not a soul about, I took the first road right and reached Coldrain Hill. I jumped from my bicycle and there below was Wood of Coldrain, my Uncle's farm. There was nobody to be seen. Maybe they are at tea, I thought, and jumped back onto my bike and started a long freewheel down the road. As I neared the road end into the farm, I noticed a light in the Wee Field, and there was the figure of Jock working with some sheep.

'Hullo' I shouted.

'Is that you, Andy?' from Jock.

'It is.'

'You're just in time; I need a hand here.'

The corner of the field was divided into small pens with square blocks of straw. Jock was wrestling with a ewe with wild, panic-stricken eyes and the head of a lamb hanging from her.

'You take her heid, and I'll see if I can help her. It's her first lamb and she disna ken whit's happening.'

I took the ewe's head, smoothed the wool around her eyes and spoke to her.

'Steady now lass, steady – you'll be all right.'

It made no difference. Jock came round.

'Look, we're going to lose that lamb. It's all twisted up inside. Your hands are smaller than mine. I'll hold her and you see if you can straighten it out.'

Off came my jacket and I rolled up my shirtsleeves. I had no idea what to do until I put my hand on the lamb's head. Then I knew. One leg was twisted up round its neck while the other was stuck at right angles. I turned the head around and the leg straightened out. I then found the other leg, brought it forward, and laid the head between the two legs. Holding them together, I pulled gently and then with a great heave from the ewe, I found myself on my knees with a lovely black-faced lamb in my hands.

'Clear its nose and mouth,' said Jock, 'and put it down for her to clean and see.'

'There's another one coming, Jock.'

'It'll be nae bother; bring it round beside this one.'

I did so, and then noticed a third one.

'It's triplets, Jock.'

'Right, gi'e her a hand. It'll no' be sae strong as the ither two.'

When I put the lamb down beside the others, the ewe smelled it and pushed it away.

'She disna want it,' said Jock. 'See that ewe in the next pen? She had a stillborn lamb yesterday and she's desperate for one. Dave skinned her lamb and put the skin in that bag ower there. Bring it out and we'll tie it onto the triplet and we'll see if she'll take it.'

We did just that. The ewe sniffed around and then seemed to recognise the skin and started to clean up the triplet. It could not stand, but she pushed it against the straw, lay down on the other side and put the head to her udder and there was wee triplet having its first feed.

When we looked into the last stall, we found that two ewes in there had managed to give birth without help and were lying comfortably in the straw with twins.

'We'll go and have a wash and a cup of tea now,' said Jock. 'Jean will soon be back and we'll have a bite to eat.'

'I'll run down to the crossroads and give her a hand with the messages while you're cleaning up. Are you going to let them know at Sandport that the lambing is finished?'

'Oh, I'll see. Maybe I'd better. The Old Boy won't sleep till he knows.'

Holidays at Wood of Coldrain were happy times. Jock played on a small melodeon and I played on a mouth organ and everybody sang the old Scottish airs as well as the 'latest'. We danced and worked: I learned all about horses, cows, sheep, and pigs, in fact, everything about farms. I was anything from five to ten years younger than my cousins were, but I was made to join in with their lives and I recited and sang and drew little sketches and pictures to please them. I was with them the day War was declared. A Sunday morning, Uncle Jim, Dave, Jock and myself had wandered, as was usual, down the long field where the cattle were grazing.

'I'll maybe book three into the market next week, if I get a chance,' said Uncle.

Up to the top of the high fields we followed the march fence. Conversation was desultory. 'We'd better wait and see what the weather's like. We could be cutting roads next week.' The view was thirty-six acres of golden yellow.

'It's ready, anyway.'

'A week like this and it could all be stooked.'

'Oh, that bit near the bottom will need another week at least.'

Uncle ran his hand along a yellow stalk, taking all the ears. Then he rubbed both hands together and was left with a handful of oats. We tasted one or two.

'Sweet as a nut and milky too.'

'Oh, aye, we'll get the scythes out ready.'

'A week o' sun and a bit o' wind and we'll get a good price for this.'

'We'd better get down and hear the news. Jean said she'd have a pot of tea on. A pity you didn't have a sheet of paper and paints with you, Andy. Isn't that a great picture?'

'I'll store it in my memory and send it on to you when I have it finished.'

We sat round the big kitchen table and listened to the wireless. Nothing was said for a time. Then Uncle spoke.

'We'll need an extra man full time, Andy, so if you like you can stay on here. We'll all be exempt.'

There were nods of approval round the table.

'They're no' coming up the road the day, and I'm going into Sandport, so outside all of you and I'll clear up in here. You can discuss in the stable and let me know the result later,' said Jean, taking charge.

I had just finished two years at the College of Art. Two more to do, a year's teacher training, and then I would be earning a wage.

'I'll carry on until I'm sent for,' I said, hesitating a little. 'They said I'd to carry on with flying training at weekends.'

Uncle spoke thoughtfully. 'I think you're right. It will please your Mother. But keep in mind there's a place here.'

My time at the College had been difficult. I had no money to live like other students. When I first started I sat an exam in Glasgow and was awarded a bursary from the Marshal Trust for fifteen pounds for four years. Consequently, my exam results were to be sent to the Trust annually. I also had a yearly train ticket from Cobbinshaw to Edinburgh, 'the ticket to cease if I failed exams.' I received a grant from Scottish Oils because my father worked there. Nevertheless, all this was not enough for Art College life and so, when Hugh, my College friend, started to go down to East Fortune on Territorial training for the Army, I followed his example. However, as I did not wish to run across mud and stick bayonets into others, I went to Drem in East Lothian to be with the Air Force. How completely innocent and naïve I was.

At Drem, I was instructed on how to look smart as I was now in a very elite section of the country's defence forces. I was taught the Morse code and given talks on the theory of flying. I was taught the ranks of all officers, how to salute, and I was told how to identify aircraft. At the same time I was learning a new language: RAF jargon! I was also taught how to keep my mouth shut. 'Walls have ears,' we were warned.

A month later, the weather being good, the harvest finished and safely stacked for the winter, I was back home preparing for Art College and waiting for my call up. Not knowing whether it would be this week or next, it was an uncertain time. Eventually, I received a letter instructing me to report down south. Farewells were said and I was off for final training.

Strangely enough, I enjoyed my first days and weeks in the RAF, first in Wiltshire and later in Cottesmore for Operational Training before moving on to Scampton. Very early on, I determined that if anything was to happen to me, it would be through no fault of mine, and so I settled down to concentrate on every little point I was told, and to perfect myself for every occasion. The complete change from the College of Art, where there was freedom to create, to the rigid disciplines of flying, guns, map reading, wireless coils, aiming and dropping bombs, and a hundred other things, was something I could scarcely believe. By the time my training was complete, I was able to take over any position when on a flying mission although I was essentially a Wireless Operator Air Gunner.

And then there was the meeting of strangers from all over the country, coming and going, hearing of people we knew, mostly students, and finding we were all very close. In spare time we kicked a ball around and exercised in the gym. I used to walk around the countryside chatting about gardens with the locals. And there was always a dance, enjoyed by everyone, at the local town.

When training was finished at Cottesmore, aircrew went off to Operational Units to fly in Hampden Bombers. These were lovely planes to fly and I have yet to hear pilots say a word against them. They were given names of sweethearts and wives and were looked after with the self-same loving care.

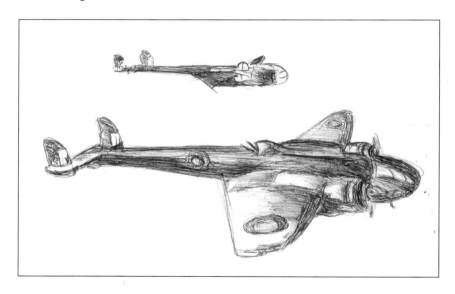

Author's sketch of Hampden Bombers

Chapter 4

'The best laid schemes ...'

There was a very friendly rivalry on the station between 49 Squadron and 83 Squadron, the sister Squadron. Football was the natural release for pent-up operational missions. In a 'friendly' one day, with three minutes to go, the inside forward was pushing towards our goal. A long sliding tackle was the only way to stop him and so in I went. I managed to tip the ball away to my left back, but got my leg where the ball should have been. The result – a very sore kick just below my knee and a badly twisted ankle. The backie booted the ball across the field to the right wing, and there was wee Jimmy Young flicking it past the opposing defender. Right down to the bye-line it went: he stopped it, did a sort of Highland Fling over it and swished it back to the penalty spot. There was Rammy, our centre, with a beautiful left-foot drive right into the corner of the net. We had beaten 83 Squadron, but I was carried off.

'Is it broken?'

'I don't know. We'd better take him down to the doc.'

The leg was x-rayed. It was not broken but I was given a week on sick leave. Towards the weekend I was hobbling around without a stick but was informed that I would be off for at least another ten days. I was called into the office, and, as was usual, I was told that it had been decided to send me on leave for a week. There would be, however, a break in my journey to go to the funeral of Ron Clarke, a friend of mine from my Squadron who had been killed in a crash on landing with a badly shot up plane. As I was to represent the squadron, I had to wear 'best blue', say nothing about operations, and just stick to personalities. Passes, ration cards and my route vouchers were ready, and I was off.

It was a smooth run to the station south of Carlisle. I jumped out and asked the porter for directions to Ron's village.

'There's a bus in an hour, twenty minutes run. The funeral's tomorrow and there's a very good small hotel at this end o' the village. Go there and they'll keep you right.'

Clearly, he was aware of my destination. A car driver approached me to say that he was taking two others to Ron's village and that I was free to join them. I checked the train time to Carlisle the next day and found that there was a connection to Edinburgh. Two middle-aged to elderly people welcomed me: Ron's relatives. They had come for the funeral and were staying within the area for a day or two.

In no time, we stopped at the hotel and with 'see you later', they were off. I went in, arranged a room and meals.

'There'll be a cup of tea in the lounge downstairs if you care to join us,' I was informed and I was left to settle in. Later, in the lounge I joined six others who had also arrived for the funeral. I introduced myself and had a quiet conversation with one or two.

One of the hotel girls came up and said, 'Mrs Clarke would like you to join her. She wishes you to come now as she is arranging the Church service. I'll take you.'

We walked quietly along the street until we entered a cottage near its end. A girl rose from the table.

'I'm Joan,' she said, 'and you are?'

'Andrew Winton from 49 Squadron. I'm here to represent the Air Force at Ron's funeral.'

Two men in the room rose. Joan introduced us.

'This is the vicar who will be taking the service tomorrow, and this is the clerk.'

We shook hands and all sat down. The vicar took over.

'The service is at ten-thirty tomorrow in church. We will then walk to the graveyard where interment will take place.'

Joan looked at me for a minute then asked, 'Do you like poetry? Do you read poetry?'

I nodded.

'Ron liked poetry,' she said in a very quiet voice. The vicar took up the theme.

'Joan would like a poem read at the service and wondered if you could do it?'

'What were you thinking of? Something short? A sonnet?'

'Yes, we'll think about it, unless you have a poem in mind.'

'If I could have a Treasury? I'll go for a walk and let you know.' That settled it.

'After the service we'll all walk back to the hotel where lunch will be served. I'd like you to sit at my table and we can talk. Will you stand at the foot of the coffin as it is lowered into the grave? We'll get you to Carlisle in time for a train to Edinburgh.'

So it was that the next day, after breakfast, I went for a short walk. When I later saw the vicar he approved of the poem by Thomas Moore that I had chosen. By ten o'clock the congregation began to arrive. I was amazed at the numbers. Everyone had the look of a person who had been hurt; they were shocked that tragedy could have hit Joan and Ron. The service was a simple one. I was introduced as a friend who wished to speak.

'We were a group that used to gather out at a hangar awaiting daily orders. We would talk and laugh and often, lying on the grass, we would read poetry. This was a great joy and you who knew Ron will know that he took a prominent part in our poetry sessions. We will miss him. Here is one of his poems.' I put down my paper and walked over towards the coffin.

> *'At the mid hour of night when stars are weeping, I fly*
> *To the lone vale we loved, when life shone warm in thine eye;*
> *And I think oft, if spirits can steal from the regions of air,*
> *To revisit past scenes of delight, you will come to me there*
> *And tell me our love is remembered, even in the sky!*

> *Then I sing the wild song it once was rapture to hear*
> *When our voices, co-mingling, breathes like one on the ear;*
> *And as Echo far off through the vale my sad orison rolls,*
> *I think, O my Love 'tis thy voice ...*

At this point I paused, and then in a quiet tenor voice I sang softly:

> *O my love 'tis thy voice from the Kingdom of souls*
> *Faintly answering, answering still the notes that once were so dear.*
> *Answering still the same old words that once were so dear.'*

I walked back through a solid silence. Not a word was spoken for a full minute as I took my seat. Then, the vicar thanked me and finished his own tribute. Six men came in, took away the coffin and we walked behind it to the grave where everyone gathered round. A short few words, a prayer, and the coffin was lowered. The service ended and we began to drift away, not quite understanding. Back at the hotel, Grace was said and lunch was served. Joan said she would see me later, thanked me for the

poem, and mingled with the mourners. I had been to many funerals, but
this was one I was not likely to forget.

Good-byes were being said all around the dining room. As the
room emptied I took a seat at a window overlooking the garden. Joan
came over and sat down.

'Jim and Mary are going up to Carlisle and will drive you there in
plenty of time for the Edinburgh connection. Your poem was just
beautiful – we had a special place and I'll go there. Are you married?'

I shook my head.

'Have you a girlfriend?'

Another shake, then I ventured, 'I'm a bit mixed up about this. I
don't want to be committed to one person – to leave her with maybe the
thought of looking for somebody else.'

She took me quietly by the hand.

'Like me?'

I said nothing.

'I'm going to tell you,' she began earnestly, 'that one person
would a thousand times wish she had been with you for a short time than
not at all. Now, promise me you'll go and see her on your leave and tell
her what I've said and arrange to marry on your next leave. Promise?'

I nodded.

'No half nods. Now promise.' She was adamant.

I nodded and said, 'Yes.'

We talked of many things until Jim and Mary arrived. I collected
my kit, paid my bill and said, 'Goodbye'. We stood close for a minute.
She kissed me and said, 'You have been very good for me. Now take care
and remember your promise. Bye.' And I was away.

There were no flaws in the journey to Carlisle and on to
Edinburgh. I sat in the corner of a compartment thinking of the past forty-
eight hours: of war, people and faces; of meetings, goodbyes and the
differing reactions that make personalities; and the outward self-assurance
to hide inward concern. Thoughts such as these were new to me. I was

glad when the train pulled into the station.

During a most pleasant spell of leave I visited my friends within walking distance and then strengthened my ankle on the old pushbike to visit those further afield. I saw Margaret on her day off at her home and we completely agreed arrangements for the future. I had three more trips to do to complete a tour after which I would be entitled to a long spell of leave. If anything happened to me in that time and I did not come back, Margaret was not to mourn, but to find someone else!

Once back at the station I was contacted to see if I would make up a crew for that evening. The rear-gunner had had a motorcycle accident and it would mean maximum effort if I went. I agreed; it would be one more trip towards the completion of my tour and that would be all to the good. After an early meal, I picked up my kit and got a run out to the perimeter, met the other three members of the crew, checked my guns and settled down for take-off. We were last to go with quite a time to wait. It was a clear night, the second last night of September 1941.

Chapter 5

Shot Down

It was cold in the tin, the rear gunner's position. I had not realised that the temperature could be so low. There appeared to be no heat coming through from the starboard engine; I must report this when we get home, I thought. I shifted around as well as I could and twisted the hot air from the port pipe so that I was blowing it around my body. That helped. The pilot's voice came through.

'Did you check the starboard tanks before take off, navigator?'

There was a pause before Pete's voice could be heard.

'You know damn well I did. You were with me.'

'Could you slip back and take another look? There's nothing coming through and the engine's dead.'

After a long minute, Pete's voice was heard again.

'All empty; must have been hit before running in on target.'

The target was the steel works in Strassburg and the German gunners were putting up a very heavy barrage. We had already seen a complete blow up ahead of us and believing in the adage that it does not

happen twice, we had gone straight in. 'Steady! Steady!' ... 'Bombs gone
... ', and we had swung away.

Two minutes later the pilot's urgent voice was heard again.

'I've done everything I can. I can't keep her up on one engine. If
anything happens to it, we'll go straight in. I think you should all prepare
to bale out. As
soon as I can
flatten out, I'll
give the word.'

As if to
emphasise his
words we were
hit a second
time. Engine
number two also began to splutter and caught fire and the hurried order
came.

'Right! All out. Good luck!'

Parachutes checked; all four were out. One, two, three, four, five,
six: I pulled the ripcord. A little strain, a bump and I was sitting in
blackness. Away to the east, a black shape slipped into the fire glow,
turned into a perfect nose-down silhouette and disappeared: the last sight
of a lovely plane.

I was in space, hanging in blackness: nowhere. I looked at my
watch, a present from my mother with a luminous dial. Twenty past three!
It must now be the 30th September. I was swinging. Try and steady by
pulling cords ... My mind ceased to function and then there was a rush of
thought: Woolfords: the farm; Art College; Dot and Jean; tennis partners;
Wood of Coldrain with Jean; Jock and Peg; my cousins; the high field;
back home to Woolfords; Granny; Cobbinshaw ... swimming ... floating.
A sickening bump on my left side brought on a fit of nausea, a pain in my
right shoulder and a dead feeling in my foot. I was very sick, and cold,
and then all was quiet again. A great silence: I passed out. Awareness

returned with changing thoughts. Where am I? Back to Cottesmore and Joan, dancing partner, singing and dancing, football, the D & P room at Art College, Hugh Benzies, my friend at College, his mother and father, cycling to Kinross, picking berries at Sandport ...

I felt my foot among branches. I was swinging again and could not see the ground. My left leg was useless. My chute was caught high up and so I began to swing again: a crashing of breaking branches and I hit the ground, left leg first. I passed out again. How long for, I have no idea, but when I opened my eyes, all I saw was a cloud of white parachute like a blanket. I pulled it down out of the tree, draped it around me and dropped off to sleep.

Wakening, I opened my eyes, lay perfectly still and wondered where I was. After a minute or so I moved my head from side to side. I was gazing at a cloud of greyish-white parachute through branches when everything came back and I jerked into life. The pain in my leg stopped me: I almost fainted. I looked to see what was wrong. No boot on my left foot – it must have been blown off – and my foot sort of twisted outwards, but no broken skin so far. I lay back to consider. First thing to sort out was my foot. I could make a moccasin from my parachute.

Fortunately, I had sharpened my small penknife when I was on leave. It cut through the strapping, strings and cloth easily. I cut several long bandages and pleated the strings, cut slits in a strapping that was longer than my foot, threaded the strings through the slits and tied it up to my leg. This was an agonising job. I then wrapped my ankle with broad strips of silk and finally tried to stand up. Sweating and cold with this operation, I managed to crawl to a clump of hazels and young spruce trees.

Rested, I began to think coherently. Hungry and thirsty, I ate one square of a block of chocolate which I had slipped into my pocket before leaving the station. As I was not going anywhere until I made my leg work, I set to with my knife. It took a long time to cut four short lengths of hazel and two longer lengths to act as a walking stick. I collected my parachute, cut long strips of bandage and wrapped the sticks in twos. The rest of the forenoon was spent in cutting up the parachute. When this was done, I stripped off, put on a long 'shirt' made from parachute and dressed on top of it.

I then stripped off my leg. As this was not as painful as the day before I was able to re-wrap it in a more tidy and steadying form and put on a sock. I tied on my two splints which were about half an inch longer than my leg. On with my trousers and, with the use of my stick, I was able to stand up. One more bandage on my arm, I hid what was left of the parachute amongst the long grass and roots in the bushes, and set off.

Progress was slow and painful. Looking upwards through the trees, I felt I was going westward and taking a slightly downward course.

Thirsty and hungry, my leg hurt and I felt I needed a bath. My misery was at its worst when I heard a voice away in the distance, a 'Howya, Howya, Howya,' automatic and without meaning. Another very slow fifty yards and then through the thinning trees was a flat green stretch of grass. Edging forward to some bushes, I experienced my first lesson in escaping: it is easier to see out of bushes than to see into them, and so I was glad to rest and watch. The voice was coming nearer. Into my picture came an elderly horse, followed by a cow, both pulling a form of plough held by an old man. It was he who was shouting to the two animals that were paying no attention but just plodding along.

In a light-headed way, I was back in Room Eight at Lanark. A quiet Wednesday afternoon with Mr M sitting at his desk reading from Canterbury Tales,

> *'Whan that Aprille with his shoures sote.*
> *The droghte of Marche hath perced to the rote.'*

On page two of his book was a line drawing of what I was seeing in front of me. Surely this was not a country at war? Was this part of the machine that had shot me out of the sky? The plough was slowly returning. I hid down to see how far it was going. At fifty yards or so, the plough was turned for the next furrow and then the old man picked up a tin pan, had a drink and started off. I sidled sideways, watched him pass with his 'Howya', hobbled to the field end, grabbed the half-empty can and gently emptied it. Nectar! As there was no bread that I could see, I slipped back into the trees.

A smell of smoke told me that there was a house nearby. Not knowing what I intended to do, I moved down through the wood to the source of the smoke: a little hovel of a house with a collection of sheds, lean-tos, carts and untidy farm equipment. I settled down to rest and watch, slowly sucking another square of chocolate.

I began to work out what to do next. 'The best way to escape is not to be caught' were the words of a lecture we had had at Operations Training Unit. But there were difficulties: I was somewhere in Germany, but unsure of exactly where: somewhere between Stuttgart and Frankfurt am Main. Would it be better to make for Basel, in the north of Switzerland and then to France, or to head further south in Switzerland? And how? In the meantime I was stuck; my leg was in need of attention. I could not travel anywhere until it was sorted. I was hungry and becoming desperate, both physically and mentally. What a jumble of choices!

My thoughts were stopped when I saw the old man with his animals returning. Everything seemed in slow motion. He drank at a trough, then the horse and cow followed suit before being led into one of the sheds. He sat down on a seat at the window. A woman appeared with a plate of food, sat down beside him while he ate. They talked for some time. When they finished, the old man gave his face a *sloosh* at the trough, dried himself with a towel on a rope and went inside. When a quarter of an hour had slowly passed, they both came out, the woman carrying a case. The man locked the door, put the key up on the lintel ledge, and off they set along the road. I watched them as they rounded a little bend and then, with my heart beating loudly, I crossed the road. For the first time in my life I intended to enter a stranger's house uninvited. I tried to tell myself that they were 'enemies', and that I had the right to do as I wished. But no! My upbringing insisted, 'Don't do it'. Yet hunger was not to be denied.

I took down the key, opened the door and entered. On the table there was a loaf of warm brown bread. I cut off three thick slices and put them into my pocket. There was a large bowl of lukewarm soup. I sat down and swallowed about an inch from the top. It was sour, but I cared not. I then tidied up the crumbs, rinsed the spoon, slipped out, locked the door, put the key back on the ledge, and staggered back towards my hiding-place. As I passed the rubbish dump I saw a bottle. Over to the water I went, washed it out, filled it with fresh water, re-crossed the road in spite of a badly complaining leg, and crawled deeply into some bushes and young spruce and settled down. Half a slice of bread and some clear water focused my mind. I promptly finished the slice, drank more and prepared a better hideout. I was tired. I wanted to sleep. I was anxious about my leg and was quickly coming to the conclusion that I would need help. I curled up and slept.

It was still daylight when I awakened. As I did not want to give myself up to the old folks, I went slowly away in an easterly direction. Dusk saw me only about half a mile from the cottage I had left. Here, an overgrown, ruined shack offered a sheltered place for the night. Growing behind the ruin was an old apple tree with several late fruits. I gathered three or four for supper, but only managed two. I settled into a corner as best I could and dozed and slept until daylight. I ate my last slice of bread, finished my water and lay thinking and stretching, trying to make up my mind. I knew I would need help, but there was a strange sort of fear. The Operational Training Unit talks came back to me: 'Try, if possible, to go in twos. The wrong move of a single person meant a shot and who was to know?' My big hope was to meet someone without a gun, possibly female. It began to dawn on me that there would be very few men around: these would be old and without guns. And then a story about the 'female of the species being more dangerous than the male,' came to mind and the old fears returned.

I began moving to the roadside, a second-class road with an overgrown ditch on either side. I sat down on the bank facing the road and decided I would make myself known to a suitable person. Resting there, I slackened off the bandage on my leg and left it so in the cool dampness of the ditch. Soon, along the road two figures came into view, a little boy and a girl with school bags. I pretended not to see them while concentrating on re-tying my bandage. I knew no German; at Lanark we had studied Latin and French, and so I began to sing quietly.

> 'Allie, ballie, allie ballie be,
> Sitting on my mammy's knee,
> Greetin' for a wee baw-bee,
> To buy some Coulter's candy.'

When I finished, I looked up. They had stopped in the middle of the road, still holding hands and so I smiled and said, 'Guid morning'. There was no reaction, just two stolid stares. I must have looked a sorry sight to both: my face with a three days' growth, scratched across one cheek; my tunic, torn along one sleeve, hanging open and showing a blood-stained rag and my trousers and homemade shoe in a sad state. I picked up a small stick and drew a rectangle on the sandy road, put a wheel at each corner and then drew a big cross in the middle.

I pointed to my arm and leg, back to the drawing and made a play as if I had a telephone, dialling numbers and speaking. I beckoned to the boy and made a movement of arms as if running, and pointed back up the road. For the first time, they started to whisper to each other. I took out my chocolate, broke off one square, cut it in two and offered it to them. The boy took it and went back to the girl who spoke quite distinctly, whereupon the boy brought it back and put it into my hand. A little more talk and the boy put down his bag and ran away up the road. I lay back on the bank, closed my eyes and sang one or two nursery rhymes and *'Sandy, he belongs to the mill'* in a quiet voice. There was no response of any kind from the girl until she pointed along the road and waved a hand. Running down the hill came the boy and his mother. She ran straight to the girl and spoke urgently. A shaking head made her stand and look at me. She pointed to my leg and spoke. I shrugged, shook my head, pointed to my mouth to show I needed a drink of water and then lifted my trouser leg to show that I could not walk. She seemed to understand, made a movement to tell me I was to stay where I was, took the hands of her children and walked down the road. After ten yards or so the little girl turned, waved and smiled and then went on.

A half an hour or so later there was the sound of an engine. An old half-lorry arrived and stopped. It was a wood fuelled engine, the first I had ever seen, and again I wondered where I was and what country this was that was conquering the continent. The woman and two men came out. All three tried to speak at once and again I intimated that I did not understand. I then tried French, slowly. The woman seemed to know as much as I did but the men drew her aside and had a short discussion. It appeared that one man would go back and telephone for help. I was to stay and prepare to go with the lorry.

The first thing the man wanted was to ascertain if I had a gun. As he began to search me, I objected by saying I had no weapon. He hit me hard with the back of his hand, straight across my mouth, shouting and saying what I understood to be that I was not to speak. As I spat out blood, the woman spoke to the man who turned as if to hit her, but she held up a hand and he stopped. He was very angry and when I tried to stand up he stepped forward and kicked me just above the knee of my bad leg. I dropped back into the ditch, my whole world swimming in a sea of pain. I couldn't see properly, but one thought predominated. If that man had had a gun I would now be dead. Gradually I began to collect my senses, but I just lay still, not moving. This new view of life was not reflected in the environment around me. I resolved to do nothing that would give any excuse for mad reaction. After a short time the driver came back. It appeared that I was to be taken to a major road. The woman and the driver helped me to the lorry and we all chugged up the road until we came to a crossroads. There we drew in and waited.

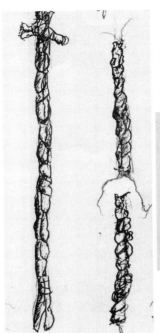

Left: Walking stick (two hazel wands tied together with parachute strips) and two splints for bad legs.

Below: Strong bag made with a strip of parachute, plus strap and string.

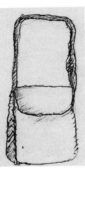

Right: A length of parachute cut out with a penknife to make an under-shirt and provide spare cloth.

Above: Sandal Mark 2 made from a piece of webbing from the parachute with nylon cord through slits to tie onto foot and leg.

Chapter 6

Arrest

Half and hour later, a smooth Mercedes drew up and a very smooth German air force officer stepped out and addressed me in American English.

'Hard luck, old boy! Shot down?'

I nodded and then I heard the words I was to hear again and again.

'Ah well, for you the war is over. We will look after you.'

As he moved to speak to my 'captors' who were obviously expecting some commendation, I spoke.

'May I make a comment, sir?'

'Yes?' he asked, inclining his head.

'That man over there hit me,' I said, pointing to my mouth, 'and I am unable to walk properly because he kicked me on my bad leg for no reason.'

'That is not a comment, that's a complaint and in your position you are not permitted to complain. However, I will speak to him.'

He went over to the three with his driver who took out a sheet of paper, wrote some notes and then had them signed. Two steps backwards, a '*Heil Hitler*' and I was ushered into the Mercedes. We were off. Nothing was said for at least ten minutes until I was told, 'You'll be taken to a doctor to be cleaned and examined. I will come back and take you to our Mess later.'

After another twenty minutes' silence, we drove into a unit where I was stripped and sent to a shower with two British prisoners of war who signalled to me not to speak. I revelled in that shower and when I came out I was given a razor and a comb. Back into my underclothes (there was a slight bewildered amusement at my long undershirt), I was given a different tunic and taken to the medical room. My arm was attended to with three clips and a bandage and then I was laid out for an expert to look at my leg. I must have passed out at this stage as, when I came to, I found that my leg was straightened out and I had a sort of plaster bandage round it. There was, however, no pain. I was given a stick and told to walk quietly. I had a quick word with the two medical orderlies attached to a prisoner of war camp who had been brought in especially to sort me out. They said they might see me again in about ten days.

A German then escorted me to the Feltwebel or Sergeants' Mess where I was asked to sit down to eat. There was an arrogant superiority around me. I got the feeling that I was considered an inferior kind of person: they would suffer my presence amongst them. Having eaten, they were strutting around with drinks, lauding deeds in the air. Then there was a call for a toast. Everyone stood up to attention. I sat still with a glass of water. I had already intimated that I was not a drinker and now made my leg the excuse to remain seated. The toast was drunk, glasses thumped down on the table while several showed their animosity at my not taking the toast, murmuring openly at my presence.

The two orderlies came in to tell me that there was a change of plan. I would be taken to Dulag Luft, a camp for RAF prisoners. As I was being ushered out quietly, I was very aware that I was glad to be out of

Feltwebel Mess. Down in the guardroom waiting for transport, the two orderlies with me spoke for the first time. They introduced themselves as Jim and Brian.

'You'll be OK in Dulag. You'll get a room by yourself for the night. Interrogation tomorrow. Say as little as possible, and you'll be back in the Main Block until it fills up and then you'll all be sent to a POW camp.'

Jim turned to Brian, 'That was close up there.'

Brian looked at me. 'Why did you not take the toast? It's meaningless to us but it pleases them. If Big Hans and his pals had been in there, we'd be carrying you out on a board. Some of them are mad. Just take it easy and keep out of their road.'

There was silence for a minute or two before Jim spoke again. 'I'm from Edinburgh. How are the Hibs doing?'

'Fine, I was there last Saturday ... '

Brian stopped me. 'That was a sort of trick question! We could have been two Jerries getting information. There are quite a few around and a lot of the interrogation rooms are wired, so watch it and play safe. Don't try to be clever. Act dumb. It doesn't matter what they think.'

We were interrupted by the arrival of a small bus with a change of guards for Dulag. We were crushed into a top corner and sat dumbly eyeing each other. The guards were all smoking but we were forbidden to smoke. Two sitting opposite us deliberately blew smoke at us. I took my cue from the lads and pretended to go to sleep. Time passed slowly and then we were stopped by guards beside a guardroom. A long straight road through a flat area, lit on both sides, took us to another two gates. All were checked again and here I was entering my first prison camp. As predicted, I was taken away from Jim and Brian and led into a small waiting room. From there I went along a corridor and into a sort of cell with one bed and one chair. A small window high up on one side allowed light into the room from a 'street lamp'. A globe in the ceiling had no bulb: I took it to be 'wired'. I rolled up my tunic and trousers into a pillow, lay down on my boards, pulled the one blanket around me and dropped off to sleep.

Wakened by a burly guard with a rifle, I was taken along to a toilet. I washed in very cold water with no soap and dressed. I was told that I was going to answer questions and that I would be given something to eat afterwards. Having combed my hair to make me look smart, I wandered along with a gun in my back into a room containing two chairs and a small table on which were papers and pens lying in an orderly fashion. I made as if to sit down but found myself looking into the barrel of a rifle in the hands of a guard. I was motioned to stand at the back wall where we stood for half an hour until another English speaking officer came in. He asked me to sit down, took out a packet of twenty Players and offered me one. He said nothing, but left the packet lying open on the table when I said I didn't smoke. He then went on to tell me that he had had a traveller's job in America and that as he was home in Germany when war broke out, he joined up with the Luftwaffe and was given a suitable job. Now Chief Clerk on the Information Board, he was to find out all about shot-down airmen so that relatives would be informed as soon as possible.

'And what did you say your name was?'

'I didn't say, but it's Winton, Andrew Sneddon.'

'And what's your Mother's name?'

'Mrs Winton. Jean.'

On and on went the questions. He took out a pre-worded postcard and carefully wrote in the home address. Putting it aside he remarked that it would be posted as soon as he had my information and then began all over again. When he began slipping in odd questions about the RAF, I sat dumbly, knitting my brows and shaking my head as if I could not understand.

'Some things are vividly clear but all jumbled up,' I began as if confused. 'I think there were four of us out on a picnic or something – we were dancing and swimming and we were all blown up into the air. Oh yes, there was an aeroplane ... ' Watching him furtively, I saw his eyes light up.

'What kind of plane?'

I thought of Jim and Brian and wondered how far I could go. I screwed up my eyes, looked at the ceiling, put my hands over my ears and began a sort of twitching of features as if to bring something back.

'No, I can't remember ... ' I stuttered eventually.

He put down his pen. 'You are an artist?'

'No, I'm just an art student.'

'Oh, I see. Where were you training?'

'In Edinburgh at the College of Art.'

'Ah, dear old Edinburgh! I spent six months there. What a beautiful city it was. I used to go out for runs and walks, taking the train over the Forth Bridge to Fife.'

At this point I made a big mistake. 'The Forth Bridge,' I said, 'that's where the first Messerschmitt was shot down.'

His chair was pushed back. He rose abruptly, took out his revolver and pushed the barrel under my chin below my ear.

'Another crack like that and I'll put a bullet right up through your dumb skull. You'll never be missed. Your mother will get a card, *"Missing on operations"* and that will be all.'

I could feel the sweat below my eyes. What would Jim say to Brian about that? I decided I would say no more. I would agree with what he said if it was suitable. As it was obvious that he had shaken me and was getting no further, he decided to call it a day. He gathered up all the papers, called the guard, and left. Half an hour later, a new orderly came in with two slices of bread, spread with a sweet red jam, and a tin mug of tea. He put them on the table and looking up at the empty light holder, he put a finger to his lips and went out. In a slit in one of the slices was a thin bit of card from one of the orderlies, *'Can't speak now, will later.'* Despite the dreadful taste, I slowly ate every crumb and drank the liquid. My mouth, accustomed to a warm soda scone with butter and blackcurrant jam, objected strongly but the hunger in my stomach won the day and so I ate all.

I took some walking exercise backwards and forwards in the room. My ankle was easing and I was managing to use two feet. As I had a desire to see more of the building, I approached the guard on the door and made obvious signals indicating that I needed to go to a toilet. He shook his head saying, 'Nein, nein,' and waved me back into the room. After a while he showed me his watch, put up one finger and seemed to think that I could suffer until he was ready. The situation, however, was resolved when the orderly came along with another guard and we were all marched into the big hut at the end of the corridor. There I was handed over to the senior British POW and left to be introduced. Pete, who had been shot down along with me was in the crowd around me: he winked and stood aside. Then Hibby, the wireless operator shot down with me, appeared, gave a casual wave and wandered away. All this was intended to confuse the Germans who were anxious to identify the various crews shot down and had snoopers who mixed with shot-down airmen. I grasped the situation, went over to two complete strangers and sat down to talk of nothing. I was then taken to a clothing store where I was kitted out with underclothing, boots, an army overcoat, a cap, a blanket and a razor. I was taken to a bed amongst some sixty others and told that I would be given cutlery and a dixie after the evening meal and that I was now registered as POW No 9673.

There was a general watchfulness and suspicion of newcomers until they were recognised by previous POWs. Then the tongues wagged quietly in groups and I was told all the various methods of living on little or nothing. For the first time, I was to learn about the Red Cross in Geneva: a parcel of food each week (when the trains were running), and fifty cigarettes (when they got through) per man. We made up a group of four and decided to stay that way until we were settled down and acclimatised to our new life.

Four days later, we were told we were to be transferred to Stalag 8B at Lamsdorf in the eastern area of Germany, near Poland. I was now doing a regular bit of walking and I was due to have the stitches out when I reached 8B as there was a good medical unit there. I had lost a day somewhere and was still very confused at times, but gradually the others helped me on to a straight course and I saw all the details clearly. I realised that they, too, were picking little bits from me and fitting them into their confusions. Returning to normal living was taking, what we thought, a very long time.

When we reported at ten the next day we were given a Red Cross parcel, a bag with all our possessions and two discs with our numbers. Those who could walk marched off; those who could not walk were to wait for transport. There were forty-six prisoners and I reckoned forty guards with guns. 'Anyone trying to escape would be shot.' This was a direct order, and so we arrived at the station. We were herded into a truck, the door slid into place, and there we sat. Twelve hours later we were shunted to another line where we were allowed out in fives to relieve ourselves, lined up, counted and put back into our truck. All evening we were moved backwards and forwards and then, at two in the morning, the train set off.

The next thirty-six hours were a nightmare. Our accommodation had a notice saying 'sixty men'. There were only forty-six of us, but each man had a bundle and, unaccustomed to such travel, in semi-darkness, needed every spare inch. We tried to settle down. No matter what position was chosen (backs to the sides, feet sticking out into the centre, knees up) it could only last for a short time. Re-making bundles to make things easier brought on short tempers and sharp replies. Then there were those who had been wounded who needed more room and help. Some wanted to eat; others said they needed the toilet. When the guards closed the door, a small roll of cardboard kept the door open at the end of an iron bar, leaving us approximately one inch of daylight. Through this space we had to pee, guiding it so that the wind blew it back along the side of the direction we were travelling. Inevitably someone forgot and we had urine blowing back into our bedroom! Then somebody suggested that we try to sleep. Some slept on left side, some on right, some on backs. Legs out, legs in, curled up, legs straight. There was a suggestion that we should try standing up! The comments on each occasion went on and on. The rattle of wheels on wearing tracks, the whistles and shouts of foreign workers at every stop and start, air raid sirens on, then off, all prohibited sleep. Some managed to curl up and doze off in short spells, but others were awake most of the time, and always the same cry: 'Water, water, a drink of water.' And so on until we were pulled into a siding. We were told that we had reached our destination and that camp guards would come for us.

As each hour went past, the grumbles and language became worse. One of the badly wounded had died sometime during the night. This caused a quietness when it sank in and during that time I spoke to everybody.

'Are any of Walter's crew here? If so, collect all his papers and personal effects so that they can be given to the new camp leader and sent home.'

Nobody moved. A quiet voice was heard.

'We don't want to touch him.'

'Alright. I'll gather them and look after them. Now, while I'm talking, let me say a bit more. We'll be out of this soon, I hope. I'm certain that each and every one of you will want to forget this journey, so straighten up a bit and don't let these beggars see you at your worst. You'll all get a drink and then we'll be taken into a Med Unit to sort us out – and you two, whether you like it or not, put a blanket over Walter and carry him out.'

I was interrupted by a voice at the other end of the truck.

'My Wop has died too, but we'll get his stuff and look after him.'

'Thanks for letting us know. Now, all we can do is try to look our best and act as aircrew should.'

A voice in a group said very clearly, 'Thanks, Scottie.' There were a few 'Here, heres', then my knees sort of gave way and I was sitting down again. This was the first time I had ever imposed myself on a group and I was a bit shaken. When Pete came over and sat down beside me I knew he agreed. An Australian Spitfire pilot touched me on the shoulder with a 'Good on ya, boy' and so I could tell I had a lot of support.

There was shouting outside, '*Raus, raus*' and the door was pushed back. The fresh air was so different. There was no rush. We had sort of agreed to carry out the two dead first, six men carrying a blanket. Two lines of guards made a road, then somebody shouted, 'Shun!' and despite themselves the Germans clicked their heels. Not a word was said as we filed out, all laden down with gear, down to a large hut inside barbed wire. On a table stood two pails of water with two mugs at each pail. Without a word, we fell into two queues, filled a mug, drank it, put the mug down for the next man and walked round to the end of the queue. Second time round was more leisurely: 'Half a mug and pass on the mug, then go and sit down.' At the end of the table stood four men in army uniform, two sergeants, a corporal and a lance corporal. They introduced themselves, told us about the running of the camp and allotted us to two different huts. They advised us to take it easy for a week. We would then meet again, individually.

Chapter 7

War Stalag 8B

The Prisoner of War Stalag 8B at Lansdorf was a large 'working' camp where parties were sent out under British NCOs and German guards to do work that did not involve 'helping the German war effort'. However, RAF prisoners of war were not allowed out on working parties. Indeed, we were confined to a special compound, and surrounded by army compounds, with double barbed wire fences patrolled by guards.

In charge of our Hut was a ground staff flight sergeant with two corporals and three or four men who had been in Greece at the outbreak of war. They had managed to reach Crete where they were captured and moved to Germany and had now been prisoners for eighteen months to two years. This group had a marvellous, steadying effect on all newcomers. They brought in all food and parcels and each day checked out the German rations for each man, seeing that everybody received what was due, which was very little. I have no doubt that this group of 'old timers' made life bearable for us and ran the Hut at Lamsdorf as if it was a RAF station.

I had a top bunk of a three-tiered unit. The palliasse was well filled with wood-wool as also was the pillow. There was one great disadvantage, however. Smoke that gathered in the evening when everyone was trying to cook a meal hung around the place for two hours until all windows were opened and the atmosphere cleared. All my belongings were kept in a Red Cross box that was guarded day and night from hungry 'mates'. Each day there was a parade when we stood in rows of five to be counted, and then we walked round the perimeter looking for weaknesses in the barbed wire.

Slowly, very slowly, the days passed. I found myself lying in longer to keep warm when the weather steadily deteriorated. A great boredom set in. At an early stage I began to think of escaping. This was no life for me: I longed to be back in the fields around Woolfords speaking with the farm workers and the miners. I wanted to run across the moor each morning, to catch the half-past eight train for Edinburgh. I longed for Saturday morning clay modelling, football in the afternoon, then a walk across the moor with its heathers and burns and grasses, singing into the fresh clean air that came down over the green fields, fishing in the Bog burn and sketching with watercolours. Yet, here I was, two feet six from a smoke begrimed ceiling wondering how I could get out of it.

There were various possibilities for escape to consider. Over or through the wire meant six cuttings: far too many. There would be an opportunity to learn German during the winter. I would then need papers: workers' permits or identification cards, discs and maps. Where would I find maps? Another option was to get out and disappear into the countryside, try to jump goods trains going westward and walk, mostly at night, to landmarks 'as the crow flies' and guided by the stars? For this I would need a compass. This would be very dangerous and I would have to consider a companion. And food. I would need a flask for water and the means for boiling and cooking, all of which would have to be acquired in secrecy. Requirements such as these were going round and round in my mind, a mind not yet completely settled from the shooting down, while trying to work out a programme. As yet I had nothing! One day, I wrote a very carefully worded letter (all letters were censored) to my Mother.

'Dear All,

I am well and beginning to settle down to a strange new life – all men living in a large hut, with nothing to do by way of a job. We play cards, and ludo and monopoly and, when we can get one, we read a book. If you get in touch with the Red X, they will organise any books which you send. Maybe you could send a wee clothing parcel – a pair of socks, one or two hankies and my old Valet razor. It has a blade that can be sharpened on a tumbler and would be very handy because ordinary blades are very difficult to find here. I'll write again next week. Regards to all when you meet them. Bye for now, Boy.'

Being allowed one letter one week and two postcards the next, we were able to keep in touch with home. The Valet razor was crucial; the handle contained a magnet to remove the blade without it touching fingers. This, I desperately needed to make a compass. Finally, after a weary wait of five weeks, there was a reply from Mum.

' … have sent off two books, a shirt and socks. Your old razor looked a bit used and so I've sent you a nice new one with a packet of blades … '

My next letter attempted a further explanation:

' … we're not allowed blades etc so just send my old Valet. Tell Alex to speak to Chubby in the science room at Lanark and he'll know why I want my old Valet …'

I was taking a chance here: censors, both British and German would have to pass this letter. For the Germans, anything that was away from 'love and kisses' was just thrown into a bin and burned. Five weeks later I happily received another letter.

> ' ... *I sent off two pairs of socks, a spare shirt, two books, your pipe and 2 oz tobacco and your old razor with a cake of soap.'*

Shaving Brush/Compass: the *author's shaving gear provided him with a compass which could be used at evening or morning when the Pole Star was*

unclear. It was never discovered on searches. The shaving brush was converted into a compass by unscrewing the base and placing a small pin into the hard putty inside. A small shape, cut from an old razor blade, was then placed on top. This could be magnetised by stroking with the small magnet from the old Valet razor handle.

The two books from my mother were very welcome: *Palgrave's Golden Treasury* and a book of *Poems and Songs of Robert Burns.* Inside the 'Burns' was written, *'Settle down now and learn some songs and poems and when you come home you'll be able to recite and sing at Burns' Suppers.'* When I read this last bit to my 'combine', one cheerful soul said, 'You'll be able to recite the whole bloody book by that time!' The following morning Pete and I were clopping round the perimeter in our wooden clogs talking of the war.

'It's going to last a long time, isn't it?'

'Too long for me,' I said. 'I'm thinking of getting out.'

'Me too. Fancy making a go?'

That was the beginning of a mutual desire which was to last until we eventually got back home some years later. We began to prepare for our escape. We were both non-smokers (except for the odd one) which meant that we could afford to buy flasks and flat backs to carry what we thought we would need. As the camp was a working camp, there was coming and going with the army personnel, and the boys were only too glad to sell for cigarettes. Then, in April 1942, we decided to try and swap identity with army NCOs and volunteer to go out of the camp in charge of a working party.

We were in luck! A staff sergeant in the Australian Pay Corps and his brother, a corporal, provided us with an opportunity. Both had been captured in Crete but for some reason they had been separated from each other and only now had been reunited. The German rule was that corporals had to go out in charge of working parties, but the two did not wish to be separated again. Two months of clandestine meetings resulted in Sergeant Andrew Winton becoming Staff Sergeant Raymond Ryan and Sergeant Peter Darwin becoming Corporal Laurie Ryan. Names, numbers, addresses were exchanged and learned, as well as where and when captured and any personal details that might be asked by snoopers at interrogations. Finally, their tunics, which looked quite good, were exchanged with ours. We slipped through the wire into their accommodation, touching hands as we passed. We slept in a strange bed and submitted our names to go out on a working party.

There was a long, quiet spell while we acclimatised with soldiers, especially with Australians. I wrote a very carefully worded letter to Mother. I knew she would know my handwriting. I explained I was an Aussie who had visited the village before the war: that I had met up with

Andrew and, as letters took a long time to get to Australia, I had adopted her as a sort of 'pen pal' and hoped she would remember me to all the 'friends' I had met when I visited Scotland – *'a trip I would never forget.'*

I had a letter almost by return where Mum said she understood, would pass on information to all my 'old friends' and hoped that we (Andrew and Ray) would settle down and keep out of trouble!

I had also to prepare my coat, slit the lapels, make little pockets filled with tobacco, and stitch them up again. A blanket had to be fitted to look like a cape. As all foreign workers wore old uniforms from a variety of countries, we would not look out of place if we were seen at darkening or early morning. My big army belt was fitted out with waterproof pockets for matches and papers for cigarette rolling. I had no maps or papers, but had a sort of memory of countries and was prepared to switch routes as suitable transport wagons came slowly along. However, the Germans chose the jobs for us to do, and we had to hope we would be landed in one near to a route south to Trieste or west to Switzerland.

It was not until June that we received word that we were to go on a party to a sawmill, somewhere in East Silesia near the Polish border. This suited us well. We left Lamsdorf, a party of thirty, leaving our details with the British authorities. After a long, slow journey in a closed-in wagon with five guards we finally arrived at a siding off the main line and were herded into a small compound surrounded by a high barbed wire fence in Neutischen. Two huts as sleeping and eating quarters, also guarded, were made available. The wise ones who had been on previous parties, grabbed the best places in the army compound, but we all settled down and made ourselves as comfortable as possible.

We were allotted jobs the next day. I was put to a woodturning lathe to make spokes for wheels. Laurie (Pete) volunteered to work in the kitchen of a house where three women cooked our meals. This was ideal for our purpose as he was able to have extras, vegetables, potatoes and an odd bit of cheese, which we needed to be fit for our plan. Two or three weeks passed very pleasantly and it was plain that some of the party would be content to stay on the job. Then, I had a stroke of bad luck.

Each morning, the works foreman checked on the setting of my lathe with a metal gauge. When he moved on, I used to tighten the setting with a large spanner which I had got from another department. This took a very small extra cutting of wood from one end of each spoke. The two boys cutting the hubs did the opposite, taking a very small extra from each hub hold, and so, when assembled, there was a very wobbly, ill-fitting wheel which needed a great amount of extra fittings before the metal could be welded into place. There were panic stations all round when this was discovered. The contract would not be met and the foreman would be blamed. Inspectors came, but as we had re-set the fittings to the correct size, we lost our foreman! Another two experts were sent in his place with an extra guard. We were given a very serious lecture and told that sabotage, if proved, meant being sent to the Eastern front or down the coalmines. We stood with very innocent faces, denying any involvement. After all, how could we be held responsible for other people's mistakes? The upshot was that jobs were switched around, a fresh supply of wood came in and we settled down to make good wheels.

I was put on to a large bank saw which cut the wood into a fixed size. After four days I noticed a shake in the footplate and thought that if I could move it a quarter of an inch, it would put a slight twist in the saw blade and that then it would break. Once broken, it took a full day to weld and no wood was cut. Down on my knees to examine the situation more closely, I steadied myself on a pile of loose chippings, skidded sideways and my arm was caught on the saw blade. My sleeve was ripped from cuff to shoulder, my arm was cut from wrist to elbow and then the blade snapped and I found myself sitting on the floor with blood everywhere. Smithy, on the next machine, grabbed a handkerchief and tied it over the wound. Then I was given a ripped off sleeve and I put a tourniquet above the elbow. The guards rushed me to the door where I tied an old towel tightly round the arm. Sometime later, I was taken to a surgery in the little town nearby, pushed by the guard to the top of the queue, sat down with my arm along the table and asked in broken English if I could move my fingers. When I demonstrated some movement, there was a sort of sigh of relief. The doctor said they would save the arm and went ahead by gathering up the skin and inserting a great number of staples. He then slapped on a pad covered with sulphur and (I thought) tar. All was neatly tied up and the guard was told to bring me back in eight days. We were then returned to the works where much discussion was taking place.

Laurie and I waited. We were told that I would be sent back to Lamsdorf. Fortunately, there was a guard away on leave which meant that there was no one to take me and, in any case, I had to go back to the doctor in eight days. Laurie said that if I were sent back, he would go too. We decided to wait for the eight days to see if I could do light work. If I could, we would be kept on. And so it was. After eight days I was taken to the surgery; my bandage and the staples removed. The arm was angry looking, but very much better. Some fresh ointment was smeared on, a light bandage dressed it, and I was sent off and told not to come back again!

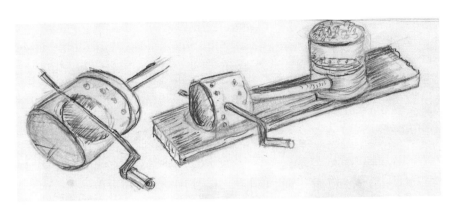

Cooking stoves: living in a large barracks with no cooking facilities, prisoners found it difficult to make the best of food parcels and so small stoves were invented. Inevitably this meant that fuel had to be found. One of the better types invented was a blower cooker which gave maximum results with least fuel. A small fan blew air into a tin and water could be boiled in minutes.

38 New Woodfords
13th July 1942

My Dear Ray.

I got your letter all right and was very glad to see that you were well and had met Andrew. We will all be only too happy to have you back with us again. Father and I were down at Motherwell on Saturday seeing Nellie & Bert in their new home. It is very nice and they were very lucky to get a house as some folk have waited three or four years for one, but of course Bert is in the Factor's office and that makes a difference. We had Chrissie home for two weeks but she is away again. She is looking well. Alex is working at the Farm, hoeing neeps meantime but expects to start the hay this week. Like Andrew he is rather thin but very healthy and brown as a berry. He likes the Farm work and expects to start at the University in October. Father is well but kept very busy, he never seems to have a minute. He was 62 on 14th June. Grannie is still working away and looking forward to having the Forth folk over for a week. We intend going to Kinross for a week. Father gets his holidays on 25th July. I had a letter from Teen last week. They were all asking to be remembered to you.

CONTINUE IN TOP PANEL OVERLEAF

TOP PANEL

Now, Dear lad, I think I've given you all the news I have this week. I am writing to Andrew too and you can compare notes. We are eagerly looking forward to having you with us again and are forever talking about you. Take good care of yourself and write to me as often as you can. Love from all Mrs Winton

FROM (SENDER'S FULL NAME & ADDRESS)

Mrs Andrew Winton
38 New Woodfords
Bobbington, West Toddles
Scotland

PRISONER OF WAR POST
KRIEGSGEFANGENENPOST
SERVICE DES PRISONNIERS DE GUERRE

AIR MAIL
PAR AVION

RANK & NAME (BLOCK LETTERS): S/SGT. RAYMOND RYAN.
British Prisoner of War

PRISONER OF WAR No.: 24413

CAMP NAME & No.: STALAG VIII B.
(E.119)

COUNTRY: DEUTSCHLAND

IMPORTANT: FOR PRISONERS IN GERMAN HANDS THE PRISONER OF WAR No. MUST BE CLEARLY SHOWN. IT MUST NOT BE CONFUSED WITH HIS BRITISH SERVICE No.

Letter to Andrew Winton from his mother addressed to his alias S/Sgt Raymond Ryan

Chapter 8

Over the Wire

When all talk of being sent back to 8B had ceased, Laurie and I decided to wait for another week to see how things went. By this time, having managed to gain some idea of where we were, we decided to go down through Czechoslovakia towards Trieste. We packed our kit in readiness for the first opportunity to 'go walking' and hung on. My arm was improving every day and I felt I could 'go' at any time.

The boys arranged a keep-fit exhibition which was to end in a boxing match at the top end of the compound. It was a lazy, warm Sunday afternoon in August 1942. The two guards were watching the show. We supplied them with some cigarettes, slipped quietly down to the bottom of the compound, pushed our kits through the wire, climbed up a corner post, placed one foot on top, jumped down, picked up our bags and we were away! A short distance of fifty yards and we were in a little hollow. We followed this for a quarter of a mile, then, slipped down a smooth bank to the side of a small river. We kept to the river, walking in and out of the water (in case of search dogs) for half an hour, before deciding to head for a wood on the horizon. Keeping to low-lying ground, we finally, at the darkening, slipped into the trees, found a good hiding hole, and settled down for the night.

We woke at daylight. Laurie slipped away up through the trees while I lit a small fire and made a 'brew' of tea before anybody was around. He returned with the news that there was a cart road at the wood edge and a great number of bushes with big red raspberries along one side. We grabbed a dixie and slipped along the road, picking berries as we went. When we had filled the pan we went back to our hiding place, had a wonderful breakfast and began planning.

The quietness around us was suddenly broken with the sound of voices: a woman and children coming along the track. They had baskets and were obviously berry picking. They stopped where we had been and then, according to Laurie whose German was fair, the woman said, 'Somebody has been here already. Maybe it would be the two prisoners who ran away. We'd better pick as many as possible in case they return.'

Watching every step, we sort of reversed away until we were far enough into the wood not to be seen. Then we travelled for half an hour looking for a good hiding place. The trees were thinning out and we could see open country and a newly planted area. The grass was long and there were torn out roots and broken stumps everywhere. Fifty yards in, we found a spot to curl up where we knew that we that we were well hidden. Not knowing when we would sleep again, we dozed off in the warm sunshine and spent the rest of the day scratching the various ants and insects that crawled in for a feed.

Sometime in the evening we both suddenly sat up and listened. In the distance there was the noise of a railway engine in stress. In no time we were packed and headed away towards the railway. An hour later we reached the track, sat down to rest and hid down the bank to await the next train. We were both on edge with time passing slowly, and then came the welcome sound of another wagon train. We had decided that if it was too fast we would simply observe, in the half light, where best to get a hold on different parts before jumping onto a moving truck. We also wished to carefully listen to find out if there was a long elevation in one direction or another. The noise was getting nearer and the train seemed to be travelling easily. We were on a long level stretch and watched it approaching. It was far too fast, but we learned a lot. We would have to go in a southerly direction for a time and it would have to be a long, heavily loaded wagon train if we were to succeed. We gathered our equipment and set off along the line. This was easy walking and we went for a long time, covering miles. Several trains passed and each time we noted speeds, noises and looked for holds for jumping and climbing: there was a variety of possibilities.

After some time we arrived at a long bend with signals in the distance and what appeared to us to be a slight rise. It also seemed that there was a long siding where wagons were left to be picked up. The snag was that we did not know where the trains were going. We found a good hiding spot on a rise overlooking the yard and decided to watch for a day. It was all very confusing as there were no nameplates or any indication as to where the different small lots were heading. The area was becoming more populated and so we turned off to a slight ridge that had trees. As we were still in Germany or German controlled territory, we had to be very careful. From the top of a higher ridge, we could see branches of railway lines going in differing directions. We chose one going off to the south-east, slipped down and got into a wagon that was returning empty, and settled there.

Two hours later, a small engine pulling six or seven empty wagons joined us and we were off! This was worth all the watching and waiting. It was luxurious to see the passing fields. Soon, we drifted into a siding, the engine was un-coupled and quietness descended. As there was no one about, we jumped out, set a small fire alight under the wagon and made warm soup with half a teaspoon of Marmite, added the last of our vegetables and bread, and enjoyed it. Now that we were sure that we were in another country, the initial stress and tension wore off and we were feeling happier about our position. We would, however, have to find food and water, but we felt that would work out. From the little hillside we fixed a course which stretched across a very broad flat plain that seemed to be covered with yellow and gold oats. We took it in turns to walk in one line, changing every now and then. Being aware that we were leaving a long line behind us, we headed on an untrue course. We filled our pockets with handfuls of the ready heads, hoping that we might boil them for porridge, or just chew them as we walked along.

Chapter 9

Czechoslovakia

O nce across the flat plain, we arrived at a more populated area, where, in a small wood near a village, we came on a fairly tidy little cottage. We watched it for some time, and came to the conclusion that the couple who occupied it were quite elderly and were working in a small paddock behind the house. Part of the field was cut and spread out to dry in the sun for hay; the scythe was standing beside a chair. The couple sat down for a rest and a drink. When Laurie walked out of the wood, they stiffened a little but did not move. He showed them his empty flask and spoke to them quietly in German. They shook their heads. He then tried French, and again the heads shook, but the woman rose, went into the house and came out with a pan of water and a mug. Laurie took a long drink, put his finger to his lips, smiled and called for me. I came out, smiling, and was given the mug, but the old lady put up her hand to stop me and hurried into the house and came back with another mug. We drank deeply, sat down on the grass, and with much nodding, set about explaining.

When Laurie was elaborating on some point, I rose and went over to the scythe, picked up the stone and gently started to sharpen the blade. When I finished the tip, I set it onto the grass and found that it did not quite fit my height, and so I slackened the wire, re-tightened the blade and drew it across the grass. Not a word was spoken. I slipped off my jacket and began scything. Once I got the rhythm, I was back at Kinross with Jock dressing the tennis court for an hour during which time I finished all there was to cut. I then re-set the blade to suit the old man, dried it off with a handful of hay, gave it a light sharpen and put it, point down against the wall, as I had seen my Grandfather do so often as a boy.

Laurie had come on apace with his communications. We learned that we were out of Germany and in Czechoslovakia. We were taken into the house to a small scullery and had a wash and shave, and then through to a living room. The main beam across the room was carved with primitive carvings, and hanging from it were numerous beautifully coloured papier-mâché folk figures. We could not conceal our delight, especially when we found that they had done everything themselves and it had taken three years. The scene took me back to the College of Art and when I was given a small piece of cartridge paper, I sat down and did a small pencil sketch of the couple sitting at the window. It turned out well, pleasing them both, and it was put away with their treasures. We then had a meal after which Laurie washed and I dried.

'That's what we do at home,' we told the couple with a smile.

The old man then produced a piece of paper, marked where we were and showed us roads and houses. He turned down the idea of going to Trieste with a shake of his head and directed us to the doctor who lived at the other side of the village about five miles away and who could speak many languages. The paper was then torn up and burned. We slept the night on straw in an outhouse and had a breakfast of porridge and an egg. We turned the hay that was ready, raked up all that the old man had cut, and set it up in small bundles. This done, we had another hot drink and a newly baked scone and went away, leaving the place as if we had never been there.

We walked for an hour or two, skirting the village and keeping out of sight. In the evening, we cut back to the roadway until we came to a largish bungalow. Hiding in bushes, we watched for some time. Judging by the number of people who arrived and went away, it was the doctor's house. After the last person had gone, we waited for an hour in the dusk.

A man came out and started tying up some flowers in the garden. Laurie approached, and said, 'Good evening' in English to see his reaction. The man picked up a stake and a flowerpot and came over to the gate. He took a very careful look around and said, 'Come in'. Laurie pointed to where I was hiding. The man nodded, went over to a small shed and beckoned to both of us to follow him. In a quarter of an hour we had learned, in four languages, where we stood. He was a doctor and had to be very careful as he had had visits from Gestapo agents with direct threats to his wife and son should he not comply with their wishes. He would have to be very careful; there had been a purge on for at least a week and people just disappeared if they showed that they did not like the regime. After a time, he very carefully watched around the house, then, went in. In five minutes he came back, picked up our gear, had another look around and took us into the house. Doors were closed and windows covered with blinds, a light was put on and a lady came in. She was introduced as his wife. Having had six months nursing training in London, she spoke with only a slight accent. When she went into another room we heard water running. Returning with a huge towel, she told us to have a bath while she prepared something to eat. Washed and fed, we gathered up the dishes, washed and dried them and they were put away.

We told them then that our uniforms of Australia were part of our escape plan and that we were air force personnel from England. This settled everything and the doctor brought out a small map which showed that we were well into Czechoslovakia. We were advised for the second time not to go to Trieste, and were shown routes to Switzerland. We were shown photographs taken in England and we promised to go and see some old friends of theirs on our return. There was also a photo of their ten year-old boy who was asleep. They did not wish to wake him as he would be sure to talk about us. We then promised to say nothing of our visit should we ever be interrogated, shook hands solemnly, said our thanks again, and after another careful look, we took our road. The lady gave us a kiss before wishing us 'Good luck.'

We walked in semi-darkness for some three hours until we decided that we were far enough away from our friends. At a crossroads where there was a bridge carrying a railway, we left the road to follow the track. The shine on the rails helped us to see where we were going and we made another ten miles before dawn began to lighten our path. Approaching a town, we looked for a place to hide and sleep. We finally found a spot where thick bushes came down to the stonework of a bridge. A quick drink, a slice of bread made into a sausage sandwich and we crawled behind the bushes, put down our blanket and dropped off to sleep.

At dawn, we awoke. It was quite cosy wrapped in a blanket and so we lay and quietly talked for a while. What next? Although we were in another country we knew we were not safe. We had been twice warned that there were many, especially in towns, who would report seeing us to the Gestapo. It appeared that many were intimidated. Family members would be taken away to work in Germany if they were suspected or known to help enemies of the Reich.

We decided that we would be doubly careful and only ask for help at lonely cottages. That settled, we dropped off to sleep again.

Chapter 10

Brno and Buchenwald

Despite the noise of trains and road traffic, we dozed and slept throughout the day. In the evening, when the world around us quietened down, we set out along the road, hoping to pinpoint a goods yard at the station. Walking quietly round a sharp bend, we were met face to face by a policeman. Out came the gun. We started to explain, but he only had a smattering of German and he made us sit down. In ten minutes, an open van came along with another two officers. They were obviously looking for someone, and here we were. Straight back to town, into a police office, and when no one understood, we were put into a cell with one word, '*morgen*', by which we knew that someone would come in the morning. A mug of mint tea was handed in and we were left alone.

We were wakened early the next morning, taken through to a washbasin where we shaved and tried to look as presentable as possible. A meagre breakfast of bread and butter and a mug of tea was provided. Someone was coming to speak with us. At ten o'clock, the Gestapo arrived, looked us up and down, and then quizzed the station officers.

After an hour or so, two armed soldiers came in and we were told we were to go to Brno, in the south, for interrogation. Following a long journey by train, we were taken to a large, stone built, round jail. The courtyard was full of gypsies with small carts and fires filling the air with the smell of cooking and smoke. Bedlam! We were marched up an open stone stair round one side of the building, into a room where eight other men lay on beds smoking. We took two of the bottom bunks, stacked our gear and lay down. We had barely settled when one of the men dropped down from an upper bunk and offered us a cigarette. He appeared to be a sort of leader and began to question us. Half an hour later, when we had become acquainted, we found that we were amongst some political prisoners awaiting trial. We got on well. They were from the town of Zlin where most of the population worked in the leather industry making shoes, boots and bags for Bata, the leather king who had shops all over the country.

About two in the morning, the door was flung open and another prisoner was thrown into the cell. He was in a sorry state and was crying. The others consoled him. It transpired that he had stolen a great deal of leather and his wife, who was expecting a baby, was also involved and was in the cell next door. Gradually, we settled down and dozed off to sleep to be rudely wakened by a guard who took out the leather stealer to see his wife. Ten minutes later, he came back – his wife needed help – was there a doctor here? We tried to turn our backs to the door but there was a long half-scream, half-howl from next room and Laurie said, 'You go and have a look.' Reluctantly, I slipped on trousers and boots and went out. The guard pointed to the door and I looked in. There was a bare bed on one side, but down in the corner on the floor, a girl was hunkered and as she half turned, I saw in the dim light a baby's head hanging from her. She looked completely exhausted, her hair was wet and her face was dripping with sweat. I rolled up my sleeves, dropped down on my knees and found that the baby was jammed.

Laurie looked in. 'Tell that spokesman next door to go downstairs and get a married woman to come up with a basin of water,' I called.

The baby's head was twisted. I straightened it and eased an arm and shoulder which appeared to have caused the trouble. I felt it only needed one strong push and so I caught the girl's eye, put up one, two three fingers and made a noise like *'poosh'*. She nodded. I took hold of the baby, did the little pantomime and with a cry and push, baby slipped down and I was left standing with it. I cleared its nose and mouth and then it was taken from me by one of two women who had come up from downstairs. In two minutes the room was different, transformed by the presence of the mother and baby. I stepped back to the cell next door just as there was a loud baby's cry. All the inmates gathered around me, patting my back and trying to shake my hand. The guard took me along to a toilet where I had a good wash. On the way back to my cell, the guard opened the adjacent door and let me look in. The mother was lying with closed eyes and her baby was lying on one arm, also asleep, in perfect peace. I had wrapped the baby in a broad bit of my parachute and I remember wondering what Mr Irving, the maker of Irving Parachutes, would think if he knew that one of his parachutes was being used as swaddling clothes in a stinking cell in Czechoslovakia.

We slept for one or two hours before being taken to an office where we had some bread and tea and were told that we were to go to Brno. The two guards in green uniform thought nothing of pushing us along. We were 'assassins'. They wanted us to object so that they could shoot us and become heroes. When we finally arrived at Brno, we were taken into a bare room and searched. This meant stripping to a long German shirt and a pair of clogs. A partition was pulled out from one wall and Laurie put on one side while I remained on the other. A tall German came in and spoke in English.

'Do you wish to confess?'

'To what?'

'To shooting a German officer in Prague.'

'I have never been in Prague.'

The attitude of the man changed. In a quiet, menacing voice he said, 'We will find out.' He went to the door and gave some directions. A guard came in with a chair, put it at the door and the interpreter sat down, saying nothing. Five minutes passed and a woman came in. If ever there was a perfect uniform, she was wearing it. I had a quick thought of Grandad's weasel. In her right hand she carried a twenty-inch whip of pleated leather. She looked me up and down and spoke to the man who called in another soldier and then addressed me.

'Who did you meet in Prague?'

'I have never been in Prague.'

This was translated and I was hit across the face with the whip. A great fear that I would retaliate came to me, but I deadened my mind and stopped. Then she started screaming, 'Praha, Praha' and each time I was hit. I began to lose my balance, but the rifle in the hands behind me kept me upright. My shirt was torn down and she began to wander around me, hitting me anywhere and everywhere and screaming words throughout. The room began to swim and slowly my knees gave way. The guard stepped in and kicked me under an arm and then pushed me up against a wall. As I fell, the partition was pushed back and Laurie was shoved in. Before he had time to answer, he was whipped across the face and the whole process began again. A wooden contraption was pushed into the room. Laurie was stood up and his arms were strapped to two upholstered arms. His eyelids were opened and a very bright light was brought up to blind him. I was then told that if I told the truth, my friend would be released. All I could do was shake my head. Then, Laurie's bindings were loosened and I was put into the wooden contraption. While my eyelids were pinned back with a sticky tape and the light brought up to blind me, Laurie was asked the same question. A shake of his head and I was unfastened. We were both unable to see properly and were left sitting on the floor. The door closed.

Ages later we were roused by a burly guard, taken along a corridor, stripped of the little we had on, and put into a small square shower room. The cold water was a great relief. It was turned off and we were left to dry. We were given some old clothes and taken to another room. From there we were thrown into a lorry and taken to Buchenwald Concentration Camp. Everything was misty, but our eyes were improving after the brutal treatment.

At Buchenwald we met another prisoner, a Frenchman who spoke English. He told us that if we went with him, he could put us on to a wagon and we would receive hot food if we helped.

Not really understanding what was going on, we went with him to another hut where other prisoners were lying around on mattresses. It transpired that each morning a long wagon was pushed around three or four huts, collecting people who had died. These were taken to long graves and covered with slaked lime and after a day or two they were covered up. Because many of the inmates disliked this job, newcomers were asked to do it before they got to know the routine. Feeling that we were not quite able for this work, we stayed in hiding under the wheels of a wagon for the day. On the second day, although still very weak, we were sent out to turn the wagon wheels, and at the other end of the track, emptied bodies in a ditch. Here, jewellery was ripped from corpses by the German guards, and teeth pulled out in their search for gold.

A few days later, a lorry arrived with three Czechs who had pleaded guilty under interrogation to the murder of the German officer in Prague. The driver was the interpreter from the cell where we had been taken to in Brno. He told us to creep into his lorry and he would cover us with crates. All went according to plan. We were taken back to jail in Brno and given back our clothes.

Chapter 11

Gypsies

Unable to climb the stairs as we had done on our previous visit to the round jail at Brno, we were put into the lower level. Through the broken glass of our window over-looking the courtyard outside, we could see once again the gathering of hundreds of gypsies but now it was clear that they were due to be moved on soon.

Two guards came into the courtyard shouting. Little or no heed was paid to them, but gradually some rows of five began to form at the gate. Others, however, wandered around saying good-byes and looking for kit to take away. Then in came a Gestapo agent. He was in a hurry, shouting and pushing and roaring, '*F•nf! F•nf!*' Just opposite our window, there was a row of four people with bags. Roaring and foaming at the mouth, the agent beckoned to one of the men to complete a row of five. The man had two small girls, maybe six and eight years old. '*F•nf! F•nf!*' came the roar from the Gestapo agent, and, stepping forward, out came a revolver and both girls were shot. There was a deathly silence. '*F•nf! F•nf!*' roared the agent again.

Without a word, the father picked up the two girls, one under each arm and walked slowly to the gate. There they were placed on a small cart and covered with a blanket. He turned and came back. On the way, he stopped and spoke to a boy of about sixteen, picked up what appeared to be a length of rope and slowly went to join the line of people he had left. When he got there, he waved to the boy who came running along the wall side. As he was passing behind the agent he stopped, and then, with all his strength, he hit him with a half brick right behind the ear. Before the agent reached the ground, the father stepped forward with a length of electric cable, twisted it twice round his neck and hauled him over to a long bracket that came out from a wall. The cable was thrown over the arm of the bracket, drawn tightly so that the agent's feet were about a foot from the ground. Swinging there, the father spoke a few words to the semi-circle of women that had gathered. One woman stepped forward with a pointed iron bar. It was pushed into the figure, pulled out, and then with a loud howl she hit him on the head. This was the signal for ten, fifteen, twenty women to attack – stoning, cutting, ripping off the tunic and tearing the body to small pieces. The boots were hauled off and the lower half of the body was sliced, cut and torn until only a bloody skeleton was hanging – and all the time there was the unearthly howl.

Two carts loaded with dried shrubbery and wood were pushed in and piled up around the figure. Then wood and old furniture was thrown on top. The father came in with a ladder and two cans. The ladder was placed against the pile and the fluid was poured down into the centre from the top. Five minutes for it to soak in and then the mother threw a lighted stick into the pile. There was a *bloof* and the whole mass went up in flames. The crowded circle gradually grew wider. The heat was so intense that we could feel it through our narrow window. Gradually, the crowd started to gather their belongings and go, but others kept coming in with more fuel, and so it went on into the afternoon when it was finally allowed to die down and all that was left was a pile of white ash. With the yard almost empty, an old lorry arrived carrying four men. They watered down the ash, shovelled everything into the lorry, swept up, and drove away, leaving the yard clean and tidy with no sign of what had happened there.

Later, we were taken upstairs to street level, where we met some of the police officers we had previously met. When, on removing our jackets, they saw the state of our arms, they apologised, saying they had nothing to do with it, and gave us a small bowl of soup and some bread. Two guards then came and took us at darkening to a train for Zlin. From there we were taken under Stalag 8B guards on another train and finally arrived back at Lamsdorf. It was October 1942, exactly a year after our first arrival at the camp. Our first attempt to head for home was over and although very still very weak, we were left with valuable experience for further attempts.

Chapter 12

Lamsdorf Again

When the Medical Officer saw us stripped, he put us into two corner beds with orders to two medic orderlies to clean us up. Our diet was to be carefully exact. He would see us in three days for a full report, he announced.

Being a very large working camp, there was coming and going at 8B not customary in other places. Cigarettes and chocolate were bought and sold. When Red Cross parcels arrived to supplement German workers' rations, most of the men rallied round to make life easier. Eventually, games and sports were organised; a full-size football field was provided with extra guards to keep everybody occupied. There were classes in progress for almost every subject, and quite a few prisoners settled down to degree courses and passed exams. There were regular concerts and drama groups, but each audience was limited to fifty men. German officers were always invited. There was also a very good secret escape committee. It kept in very close touch with all who wished to escape or who had escaped, and were prepared to help hundreds with papers, permits and maps. They were able to give guidance as to various routes and even had very secret outside contacts for special escapers.

Once we had recovered from our Buchenwald ordeal we were soon in good trim and felt fit to 'go walking' again. Time was passing quickly and we spent five or six weeks entering into camp life. All the RAF members had been drafted away to Sagan and so we remained as Australians. We were, however, denied by the Germans the right to go in charge of a working party. Then there came the order that all non-working NCOs were to be moved away from Lamsdorf to a specially set up camp at Hohenfels. When we found out exactly where this was, we could not believe our luck. 383 Hohenfels was lying between Nuremberg and Regensberg, one hundred and twenty miles from Switzerland – ten nights' walking distance at twelve miles a night! The old longings returned: Scotland; the moor and all it meant. I had no doubt that I would soon be on my way and started to work out an escape programme even before I had seen our new destination. We were told that the camp was escape-proof, but we had heard this before and had proved it wrong. Everybody was to be thoroughly searched before going into the new camp and therefore elaborate plans were made so that we could take in what we would need to organise our next escape. As all clubs looked after their own equipment, papers, books, and paints for cultural use were carefully packed, under supervision, in very flat wooden boxes, and sent off a fortnight earlier ahead of the train.

In order to receive proper medical attention we were put back into the Hut we had previously occupied but while we had been away, all the RAF personnel had been moved by the Germans to a new camp at Sagan for shot-down RAF prisoners. The Hut leader, an Australian Sergeant Major, eyed us suspiciously and then told us bluntly that we were not the Ryans. He knew Ray and Laurie personally and wanted to know what had happened to them.

I told the RSM coldly that we were airmen trying to get back to Britain and that we were part of the war in order to fight the Germans and not the Australians. He could, if he were dissatisfied, seek confirmation of our identity from the Senior Medical Officer who was also Australian. I explained that the Ryan brothers had encouraged us to change identities with them and that they were, without doubt, in the new camp. As far as we knew, they were quite happy with their lot.

The RSM then told us that he, and most of his men, did not agree with escaping. He believed that the Germans were only too glad to impose sanctions if any of their number escaped, and in any case, they would not succeed in making it back to Australia. I informed him that we had direct orders to escape and that he would just have to bear with us. At this point, the Medical Officer entered and we had to move away. What he said to RSM we will never know, but we found our new companions to be very generous and we fitted in well with them from then on. Australian NCOs were mostly non-cooperative workers, but in any case, because of our escape, there was no question of our being listed for work outside the camp.

Food Parcels arriving: *every parcel counted! In 1942, the Red Cross in Geneva organised a Food Parcel delivery on a regular basis to each prisoner in camps. Adding the contents of these to 'workers' German rations, POWs made some wonderful meals. In groups of three or four, with a homemade stove, wonders never ceased. When Food Parcels stopped later on, many prisoners were unable to cope on German 'non-workers' rations and were very distressed and disconsolate.*

Chapter 13

Hohenfels

On a lovely warm summer day in 1943 we duly arrived at Hohenfels to find that it had been originally built as a holiday camp. It was made up of individual huts to accommodate twelve in two-tiered beds. There was a table and benches on which to sit: nothing more, nothing less. Although there were wood-burning stoves, there was no fuel. The huts were set up on wooden piles in rows of ten. Most of the camp was flat, but one end was deep, saucer shaped, and there was a row of huts on higher ground round the edge. The bottom huts had much longer piles, and as these were all covered in, it provided us with a lovely cellar. One look around and we drifted up to one of the top huts nearer the woods surrounding the saucer rim. We felt that here it would be more sheltered. It also was an excellent spot to keep a watch-out should we be involved in any illegal activity.

After a week or so, we managed to settle into combines of cliques and groups in the huts of choice. The escape committee very carefully selected men who knew each other to be together, if possible, and who would co-operate with each other. Sam Floyd and Old Bob Stanley, both captured at St Valery and both in the Royal Engineers, were in charge of all the work. It was decided at a very secret meeting that we would build a tunnel from our hut. Trigonometry surveyors drew up plans, worked out angles and we, the diggers, memorised and then destroyed all the paperwork. The big snag was that we had no tools, but we had all winter to work and so we settled down to see what could be done.

Carrying in the mint tea

Red Cross parcels were banned at this point. We had previously been warned that parcels would stop if it were found that tins were being used in the digging or construction of tunnels. The hoarding of food was also forbidden although hoarding was almost impossible as German rations were very meagre and getting lower as each week passed. A group of foreign workers, mostly French, came round the camp two days a week cutting long grasses around the double fenced barbed wire and keeping the area clear so that guards could see everything that was going on. While two German-speaking prisoners distracted the guard, a fair bit of trading was conducted with the foreign workers one way or another. A small garden trowel cost twenty or thirty cigarettes, while a long-handled spade, pushed quietly under a hut from the dustcart, was acquired for a hundred and fifty. Good wire cutters and hammers and other tools like chisels all had their price and soon the 'X' club had enough to begin work. Hiding places were made in all corners of the camp.

Post arrives at Stalag 383: painting by a POW

The Germans had brought in an expert gang of 'stooges' who had the right to wander everywhere, to look through windows and walk into huts as they pleased. A plan was devised with a number of volunteers to look out for any of these stooges and know where they were at any time of the day. Signals from one hut to another, criss-crossing streets unknown to the Germans, gave time for forgers to clear away their inks and papers, maps and jacket-making materials, so that when a 'ferret' walked into a hut, he would find groups of two or three lying reading or playing cards or dominoes. Sometimes the 'ferret' was even invited to join in.

Once we had reached the stage of having a cigarette and a cup of tea and a biscuit with our foreign traders beyond the wire, we got down to doing sharper deals: an earphone for a little crystal set which I was making for example. When I first heard a clear English voice saying, 'This is London with the news,' the heavy cost of the crystal set was well worthwhile. Sometimes the reception was not very clear, but generally, at some time or other each day, we were able to hear how things were in the outside world.

The floorboards of the hut were long, stout boards over the length of the hut, but some short lengths fitted into the space under Tim's bed. With no desire to escape, he made it his contribution to suffer the inconvenience of moving out and in every time we wished to work. A quiet, placid man from Devon or Cornwall, he was a Time and Motion expert. 'Keep me supplied with a good book and I'll lie and read any time the snoops come in,' he offered. He got the timing of 'bed out, boards up, men out, boards back, bed back, old boxes flung underneath, Tim reading' in eleven seconds as the door opened following a warning. Someone described the activity as being 'like changing tyres in the pit at a Grand Prix'. Then Tim had the brilliant idea of making the trapdoor on a frame with irregular ends. This meant that only one movement was needed to lift the floorboards; and this knocked five seconds off our time. We were rather pleased with that.

When digging started, it was found that there was little or no clay and plenty of sand. This meant that we had to have a stock of wood to build the tunnel. It also meant that the disposal of earth had to be handed over to a team of volunteers. Long narrow bags were made to fit inside trouser legs. These had an opening top and bottom. The lower one was tied with a pull-string which allowed the sand to slip out whenever the wearer wished. Tons, yes, tons, of earth were carried away by the earth moving team and lightly spread under friendly huts when there was snow on the ground.

Stalag 383, Hohenfels: the 'lit-up' view from the tunnel

The entrance under Tim's bed had a two-foot square frame with a tightly fitting wooden lid. On the top of this lid there was a light tray covered with dry clay and sand. When this was put level with the earth, it was very difficult, even with a good torch, to tell that there was a construction underneath. The vertical hole dropped down for some ten feet, and a light ladder was constructed by hand with three or four steps. At five feet down, the entrance of the tunnel began. This ran horizontally for six feet and then continued at an angle to take us to the surface which was about forty yards away.

Working on the actual tunnel was very hard work. Even when Red Cross parcels were coming in at one per week, it was felt that two hourly shifts were enough, and twice a week was a 'stretch'. Following every shift, Sam and Bob went down to prop up the tunnel. When food parcels ceased, the food on German rations was barely enough to keep us going. Nevertheless, gradually, if a little unsteadily, the hole kept creeping along until it was hoped that by springtime we would be able to begin 'running'.

Prisoners' Art Exhibition

Art classes at Stalag 383 had a dual purpose. While the Germans liked to see the prisoners working, art classes also afforded an opportunity to produce escape papers. Despite very strict supervision the author managed to sneak in inks and paints to forge passports.

Set for HMS Pinafore designed by the stage crew at Stalag 383

Painting of a cellist prisoner of war at Hohenfels

Chapter 14

Out and Away

It was March 1944 by the time it was calculated that the tunnel reached past the double fence. A thin pointed stick was quietly pushed up through the tree roots and its position noted. A yard to go and an exit could be made similar to that at the entrance but with a different lid. This one would have green grass on top and it would be fitted on to two wooden brackets. When placed in position, the exit hole would be hidden and we hoped the tunnel could be used for future escapes for which a regular, controlled timetable was visualised. The fifteenth of March was chosen for the first escapes. Laurie and I were third and fourth to go.

Crawling along the tunnel for what I hoped would be the last time, I kept telling myself to calm down. My insides were all springing and then I saw the small green light which meant that the guard on the wire was walking away from the exit. Into the chamber, up two steps, out with my packs and then I pushed up my head: I had a worm's eye view of the camp. Lights and shadows were everywhere. Out into the hollow, I gave Laurie the all clear while the guard was having a chat with his mate at the other end of his beat, picked up Laurie's kit, and we vanished into the darkness of the wood.

We had no idea what lay beyond the trees, but after a tentative two hundred yards we came to a road. With stars and compass we set a course and found that the road seemed to be heading in the direction we wanted. Anything between five and ten miles would be enough ground to cover before beginning to look for a hiding hole for the day. We had not gone far when there was a sound of a shot behind us. Although this put a damper on our mood, it made us step out a little faster. Our aim was to reach the Danube, cross it and follow the wide valley on the south side, when we would edge our way to Schaffhausen and then into Switzerland. The river's system caused great trouble: some of its branches ran north, some south and west, and towns seemed to be situated on both sides with guarded bridges. On a good day we skirted Donauworth, by-passed Ulm and brazenly walked through Rein, two towns fifty kilometres apart. There was a prison for under-age murderers in Rein. They were a grim lot crawling in a field, thinning turnips, I think, and weeding. The guards, with guns, followed them around, stepping on their hands on the ground and thumping those who objected. We watched from a hiding place for some time and then slipped away, thankful that we were not in that position. A long detour around Augsburg eventually took us into Black Forest country.

I had not been feeling well for some time. Our purifying crystals had been finished for a day or two and I think I had a touch of blood poisoning. This was producing huge boils, which were slowly tiring me. A day or two resting would do no harm and so we settled down into a dry corner. When on the second day we heard a noise in the trees, we picked up our gear and hid, scanning different directions. A figure came down past our den, hesitated and sat down. We recognised him immediately as an Australian who had worked with us in the tunnel and, indeed, had been in our hut. Leo was a loner from North Queensland who had had a banana farm and had shot alligators for a living before the war. He had been following roughly the same trail as we had taken, and now, as we were all one again, he felt he would like to travel with us, especially as he, too, was out of tablets and was having to boil every drop of water.

We walked on for another hour and came to a track that led to a house. Following a pow-wow it was decided that I could not go on. Laurie and Leo then admitted that they, too, were very groggy and would need help. Smoke from the chimney meant that someone was at home. We knocked on the door, took two paces back and sat down. A woman answered our knock. Laurie spoke quietly to her. Without a word she took a long pole to which she tied a white cloth and stuck it into a hole at the side of the house. She then came back and stood with folded arms at the door. None of us moved or spoke. In five minutes a man appeared; he was in the green uniform of a woodsman. He carried a gun, but made no movement to use it. He spoke with his wife and then turned to Laurie. Five minutes of explanation and the woodsman nodded and spoke to his wife. She went in and returned with a jar of water and a mug and gave us all a drink. Meanwhile, the man explained that if one of us made to escape, he would just shoot one of the other two. We nodded to show that we understood and smiled. He then explained that he was going into Munich and would take us to the police. Again we nodded, but no smiles. We were put into the van while he and his wife sat in front.

We finally arrived at a police station on the outskirts of Munich. It was full up and the three of us were put into the one room for the night for which we were pleased. It was a dirty, stinking unit and when the police saw our condition, they arranged that we should be taken elsewhere in the early morning. At five o'clock, we were loaded into a wagon with some boxes and two officers with guns in hand and duly arrived at a very large, stone- built building. We were received by two monks in long grey dress, one with a smattering of English. We were put into a large cell and signed for like the boxes. The police then departed. We sat down on chairs and waited.

Sunlight was streaming through high-up windows when there was a quiet knock on the door and two monks appeared. The one who spoke English asked if we were armed in any way. We said that they could search us if they wished, but we had nothing. He smiled gently and then he went to the door and brought in a tray with three bowls of gruel which we drank very slowly. Leo then said he would like to go to the toilet. The monk with the tray went off and came back with a large chamber pot and spoke to the other, who said to us, 'The doctor will see you when he comes.' The pot was put down at the door and they left.

We sat in silence, amazed. It was incredible. An Australian, a Scotsman and an Englishman sitting in a padded cell somewhere in Bavaria, not knowing whether we should laugh or wake up. The slide on the door slipped open: two eyes looked in, then the door opened and a hand came in, took away the pot. The door was closed again. Laurie let out a long sigh, 'I don't believe it!' And not fifty miles away where bombers were dropping high explosives on factories, railway lines and engineering works, people were dying.

It must have been about midday, when, preceded by a knock on the door, the English-speaking monk came in with a small, old man who introduced himself in very good English as a doctor. When we told him our trouble, he said, 'Ah yes, you have been drinking from our rivers.' We all nodded.

'Then we'll soon mend that,' he said confidently.

We were given a little white pill and a drink of water.

'You must not drink water without boiling it. There are many bugs around,' he warned.

He then looked at my side, raised his hands in horror and asked for hot water. When it came, he carefully washed around, muttered something about hospital and asked for a bed. 'Rest, rest, rest,' he said. Then he took a square cloth, folded it and smeared it with yellow ointment, folded another with sulphur ointment and laid them over my open carbuncle with the remark, 'That will pull out all the poison, but you must rest for four days and eat all the gruel you get here.'

When we explained that we were going back as prisoners, he thought for a minute.

'Ah, I have it. Hohenfels, eh?'

We nodded.

'There is a change of guards there. The new ones have come back from the desert and I have three wounded in an ambulance. You can go with them and see your own doctor in the camp. I will write a letter for you. The new guards are good fellows.'

And so it was to the letter. Three days later, and about six weeks after our departure, we arrived back in Stalag 383, were handed over and were put straight into a cell for interrogation the next day. The cookhouse boys rallied round and sent over a pan of thick vegetable soup and three spoons.

The following day, two guards with guns came and took us to the German Headquarters where we met the new Commandant. Every word, which we now understood, was spoken through an interpreter and therefore we had time to think of our answers. It was difficult when the interpreter gave slightly wrong answers to questions. However, after a long drawn out trial, we each were sentenced to twenty-one days in Straflager, the punishment block of the Stalag. Laurie and Leo were to start immediately and I was to begin after I had been to the Sick Bay. We were to have three days on bread and water, then one day on soup. As we were given extra bread on lean days, we were able to keep some for our return to camp.

I was taken to see a doctor, an Australian. As it was four days since I had been mended, I was laid out and the poultice carefully lifted. The Major looked at it for a time.

'I see why you had to give up.' Then to an orderly he said, 'Clean it up a bit and call me back, Joe.'

Joe went away and came back with a bowl of water smelling of disinfectant. He stood and looked at it in amazement.

'Jesus, where did you get that?'

Half an hour later he sent for the doctor.

'Seven heads, Sir, but none of them leaking,' he announced.

'Good. Now cover it lightly with a bit of gauze. We'll give it some air. Half a pint of barley water every half-hour and a plate of gruel and some vegetables every two hours.'

Joe came from Shotts in Lanarkshire. He was a sergeant in the Cameronians who had volunteered to stay with the wounded from St Valery. On the second day, he spoke quietly.

'I know you're not an Aussie, but I'm curious, and if you tell me, I'll not bother you again, but if you don't tell me, then I'll be wondering and maybe I'll start asking around.'

I took Joe into complete confidence and told him everything. He knew the district at home and we had probably played football against each other in school teams.

From then on my condition improved quickly and after six days I joined Laurie and Leo in Straflager. Time served, we settled down once again to camp life and learned the story of the shot we had heard as we had escaped from the camp.

Chapter 15

Return of the Ryans

Eric Dominy had been number twelve to go. A fluent German speaker, he meant to go by train to Basel acting as a lawyer to try a case. When he reached the exit of the tunnel that night two months ago, there was a change of guard and so he was held up. He just sat waiting patiently for the signal to go.

Outside the camp, on the upper path, a soldier was making his way towards the barracks. Tired, sleepy and half-drunk, he came to a clear view of the camp by night and settled down to relieve himself. Just dozing off, he was suddenly aware of a man coming out of a hole two feet away. Eric, who had been given the all clear on the camp side, took in the situation at a glance, picked up the rifle, which was leaning against a tree, and motioned the soldier to stand up with hands around the trunk and his trousers around his legs. The one thought in his mind was to hide the tunnel exit. He shouted down to the next man, 'Clear the tunnel, it's been found. I'll try and keep this end clear.' So saying, he carefully put the cover back on the exit, ruffled the grass all around and dug the bewildered soldier in the back with the rifle and told him to start walking.

The man had no idea what was happening. Here was a civilian ordering him to walk (Eric was wearing a home-made suit) and he could not understand what was being said. He was from far eastern Europe and spoke in a different language, and so he decided in a maudlin way to do what he was told. Eric explained slowly that he wanted to go into the camp and wished the soldier to take him in. When the man nodded, Eric fired a shot, which we all heard, handed the rifle back to the man, put his hands in the air and started walking to the main gate. His plan might have worked, too, but two German sergeants, returning from a night out came round the corner of a hut and asked what was going on. Eric quietly told them that he and the soldier had had an argument and he was now being escorted to the camp. In the half-light, one of the Feltwebels peered closely at Eric.

'Take off your glasses,' he instructed. When he did so, '*Ach so,*' said the sergeant, 'the keep-fit expert?' he added triumphantly.

Eric nodded. The week before he and two others had given a demonstration as part of an act in a concert. The sergeant, also a keep-fit fanatic, had been at the show and now recognised him in his new guise. Out came a revolver and the whole party moved into the German guardroom. Eric was sentenced to fifteen days in Straflager for his part in the action and I heard his whole story from him when I landed in the next cell when I left the Sick Bay.

His unselfish act of going back to the camp gave the escape committee time to clear most of the tunnel wood, wire and other bits and pieces and store them elsewhere. The guards could not understand how he had got out and for two days they went round the wire looking for a break. Then they found mud on Eric's clothes and realised there was a tunnel. Two more days probing the ground around the camp with long pointed irons and finally one of them found a hole. The parts of the tunnel where the shoring wood had been removed had fallen in and so the guards were able to trace where it began and ended.

The hut inmates stood to attention with innocent faces when the discovery was made, but there was no direct proof that they had anything to do with it. They were allowed to lie down with their books and listen to Davie Laird and his Band, who unexpectedly began playing songs which had been used as a warning when the tunnel was being dug. Davie, from Dundee, who had a beautiful accordion sent from Geneva was part of every concert. Two other learners had smaller instruments sent but Davie was recognised by the Germans as a tutor.

About a month later, an announcement was made on morning parade that the two Australian brothers were to report to the German Commandant after parade. An interpreter was to go with us as a witness. We duly arrived, wondering what we had done, and were put into an interrogation room with the usual partition. The Commandant was sitting at one end and he called Laurie in and began the usual questions. I sat near the partition to hear what was going on. 'What is your name?' 'What unit were you in?' 'Where were you captured?' 'What camp were you in?' and so on and on. Then he took up a new line.

'What is your mother's name?'

In quite a clear voice Laurie answered, 'Mrs Ryan'.

'Her first name?'

In a raised voice he answered 'Mary'.

'You have sisters?'

He needn't have said so many, but Laurie said, 'Three'.

'And what are the names of your sisters?'

'Rose, Lily and Daisy.'

'Ah, yes, and you are Corporal L Ryan? Bring in the brother'.

I sat still as if I had not heard. Laurie was put against the wall and I was taken in to stand in the middle of the room with my back to him. The same questions began: name, rank, where captured and to what camp and so on and on. And finally, 'You are Staff Sergeant Raymond Ryan?'

'Yes'.

There was a pause, papers were shifted and compared and then, 'Ach, so. If you are what you say, who are these two gentlemen?' He made a signal to the door and in walked Ray and Laurie. We stood and looked at each other. Then I turned to the interpreter.

'Please tell the Commandant that the two gentlemen are the Ryan brothers from Australia, and we are two members of the Royal Air Force,' I said.

Having had my words translated for him, the Commandant sat for five minutes writing notes and switching cards and papers.

'The Ryan brothers have already been in Straflager for ten days and so they will go back and join their comrades in this camp. Flight Sergeant Darwin and Flight Sergeant Winton will remain with the Air Force personnel in this camp, but are sentenced to Straflager for fifteen days, starting today. That is all.'

We turned to go out, but before we reached the door, I said, 'Halt! About turn!' We did this and I took one step forward and gave him a real RAF salute. 'About turn!' And out we went. I was certain that there was a slight smile on the Commandant's face.

Outside we touched each other. 'See you in a fortnight.' Then I got a boot in the rear and a wallop on the shoulder and neck from a guard, with the advice 'No speaking' and we marched off in opposite directions. Straight into the cooler and Pete said, 'I hope they make this a soup day. I'm starving – and don't answer back. That guard was just egging you on to retaliate and you know what that means.'

I was put into the cell I was in when we came back from the tunnel escape. As we had been taken in after parade, we were unprepared. Pete was studying for his degree and wanted a book sent in. I wanted a pencil and paper to do some drawing. We managed a note when the first food came in. Fortunately there was some tobacco up the electric wire pipe and we had some papers for rolling and matches in the belts which we wore most of the time.

The unexpected call to the Commandant had upset our programme: we had not completed plans for another escape should the occasion arise and the time of year was becoming unsuitable for escaping. Food was becoming scarce in Germany and the rations we received daily were beginning to lessen. When Red Cross parcels failed to arrive there would be no surplus and no cigarettes and we would have to replenish what we used in the cells. Nevertheless, it was pleasant to roll a thin cigarette and lie back and blow smoke rings up through the narrow flat window. This gave the guard an excuse to beat me up! I had just finished a thin weed when the door window clicked and in came the guard who had kicked me outside. '*Rauchen*, smoking,' he was roaring. Lying on my bed, I watched the last smoke ring disappear through the window, then I turned sideways and said, '*Nein, nein*.' This set him off. Walking round the cell sniffing and shouting, he was beginning to froth when he leaned down, grabbed me by the shoulder and pulled me to the floor. When he began kicking I got to my feet, but he started slapping me across the face and neck. He had no gun with him and I considered giving him a return punch, but fortunately resisted. He seemed to have something against airmen because he screamed, 'Air force, air force, smoking, smoking', all in German, of course. Eventually, I managed to work my way round to the stove grill and shouted through it, 'Get word to the Guard Room.'

Immediately every prisoner began to bang his door and shout through the grill. The other guards came running, opened my door and pulled the mad man off. By this time, he was trying to choke me. It was a relief to see him go. Later, the sergeant came along with an extra drink of water and told me to write out a full report. The man would be sent to the Eastern Front and I was free to send an account to Geneva if I wished.

Straflager: The author can be seen under the central window.

Straflager was usually full. Petty crimes (such as smiling at any girls who happened to pass outside the wire) or any behaviour that displeased the guards merited a penalty of three days. Exercise, walking at slow pace around a small, enclosed area with a guard every ten yards, was limited to one hour in daylight. The stovetops between cells were metal, squared off into sixty-four 1" squares. This made an excellent draughtboard, and so prisoners in pairs collected round or square pebbles for the game. Smoking was forbidden, but one of the first days in the cells was spent jamming tobacco up the pipe that carried the electric cable to the switch. Cigarette paper was tacked into the coat or jacket lapels and so a nice quiet puff was taken when guards were at the end of the corridor. Some were expert at sending smoke rings up through the little ventilation window. Serious students who were studying for degrees would sometimes offer to swap three or four week sentences for peace to finish off exams, and most were successful.

Chapter 16

Away Again

Back in camp, time passed slowly. I set up an art class and was swamped by would-be Picassos. I did not mind this as I had enough time for my map making and calligraphy and an occasional portrait. Gradually, however, I got a very comprehensive escape outfit ready. Just as well. Out of the blue came the chance to be off 'running' again.

It was now August 1944. For some time the Germans had been warning us that food was scarce and that we would need to make potato pits for the winter. Back at the Wood of Coldrain, my uncle's farm, I had had expert tuition from Auld Davie on how to preserve vegetables of all kinds, potatoes especially, and so I was chosen to go out and demonstrate how to store the potatoes. This was good. We dug the long trenches with water drainage and then the women came in with creels full. I showed them how to build up the potatoes into tent shapes with the long ones lying on top so that moisture would run down. After two or three days, depending on weather to keep them dry, straw was brought in. I was at a loss here because there was very little straw available. Wood-wool had to be used instead. However, by pulling it and keeping it as straight as possible, the wood-wool was laid along the potatoes like the low tiles on a roof. Another row was put down covering the top of the first row and so on until the top of the triangular pit was reached. Each row was pinned down and once it had settled, the loose earth from the trench was built up on top. The earth began at ground level and was built upwards, six or seven inches thick, and was patted down to make as smooth a surface as possible.

The work party had been in progress for some three weeks when we were told that we should finish off as there were no more potatoes. 'Tomorrow will be your last day; you have done a very good job,' we were told. The following day, a party of twenty-one assembled at the gate. The guard, we were pleased to see, was Dopey. He checked us out for numbers and we set off singing 'Hi-ho, hi-ho, it's off to work we go.' When we reached the pits we did a bit of scattering around tidying up and finishing ends. When things began to look good, one or two at a time slipped off into the trees and when Dopey said, 'Finish', only fifteen were present.

As Pete was getting on to exam time and did not wish to go, I was with Eddie Ramage, an army sergeant. We calculated that we could jump a wagon, or if lucky, we might slip into one at the railway station two miles down the road. We reached a ditch leading to the station in half an hour. There was nobody in sight, but an engine was linking up with a row of wagons: we were in luck. We slipped along the ditch, climbed cautiously up the bank, up the blank side of the second wagon, one leg over the top and dropped down out of sight.

'Tickets, please,' said a voice.

There was Henry in one corner, Percy in another.

'We're off on a picnic,' I said, 'would you like to join us?'

'We've already joined.'

The wagons began to move and we were off. Where? We had no idea, but it was lovely to be running south. We shunted at two or three little stations and picked up more wagons. When it was obvious that we were going to finish up in a big marshalling yard, we decided to slip off at the next small siding. Very conveniently we drew into a siding that had an open side leading to a plantation of bushes and trees. When we stopped, we took our time. Percy jumped down, crossed over to the wood, had a good look round then gave us the all clear. One by one we crossed into safety and had something to eat. We were following a small river and then suddenly as we turned a corner, there ahead of us was a large river. As we sat down to discuss our position, we could not pinpoint where we were or identify the river in front of us on our maps. Somewhere the railway would cross that water which we knew would mean a bridge, but it would probably be guarded. Somewhere that water would go into the Danube. It might be easier if we were to head north and cross where it was smaller. 'There's another solution,' I said. 'If any of you can row, we'll slip along until we find a small boat and go across in darkness.' The light in the eyes of Percy and Henry showed agreement.

We tossed for direction, turned right and found a small rowing boat tucked into some bushes which was tied with a stout chain to a pole in the sandy mud. I sat down on the bank, knees bent, and doubled up. With one hefty kick, the pole snapped off at ground level. I grabbed the pole and chain and drew the boat into the side. As there were no oars or rowlocks, we decided to use the tying-up pole. By wiggling it at the stern, we could create some movement and the current would take us downstream. After making sure that the boat was watertight, our gear was loaded into the bottom and we sat two on each side.

Darkness was falling rapidly and a strong push on our pole set us on our way. We had kept two old blankets out and when we were nearing a bridge we covered ourselves up and allowed the boat to drift willy-nilly. Fortunately, bridges were few and we must have travelled miles on our way when we realised we were coming to a more populated area. By dint of pole movement and use of current, we managed to slip into a quiet little bay where we unloaded and said goodbye to our craft. We took the chain off and gave it a strong push out into the deeper water and watched it swinging on its way.

We crossed a narrow field towards a wooded hillside. On climbing the hill we could see that we had arrived at a forest area with thick growths of shrubs and trees. It had started to rain. We looked for clumps of thick spruce and, halfway up the hill, we found a suitable spot. We hung blankets around three sides by tying corners to trees and gathered enough dry twigs to start a fire; as it was just three-thirty we considered that there would be nobody about. With a good red blaze going, we put potatoes into the ash and boiled water and made porridge. After eating, we sat around the fire with heavier branches burning and dried off our outer clothing and the blankets. As a strong wind was drifting heavy rain into our three trees, there was no question of sleeping there, and so we packed up while we were half-dry and set out into the deeper wood hoping to find some bigger trees where we could shelter. Heavy rain and black clouds obscuring the stars made travelling difficult. We had to stop frequently, get out the compass, pinpoint a thinning in the trees and make a beeline for the light. As I was more used to this form of navigation than the others, I took the lead and stepped out energetically with three in a line to follow.

Suddenly we came to a really good place. A small burn was running down the hill, taking in all the moisture: it dropped under some flat branches into a hollow and the rain, which was beginning to stop, had scarcely wet the area, so thick were the branches near the ground. I dumped my kit instantly.

'I want three or four flat stones in a small circle. Gather a good handful of dry brown twigs, lay them out on the stones, then heavier branches from the bottom of the trunks. Two hands on a branch and give a sharp downward tug.'

I demonstrated and within minutes we had a good fire going. The smoke going straight up could scarcely be seen. The blankets laid out around the fire and our wet clothes laid out on the low branches completely hid any sign of the fire. Percy and Henry took a walk around the place and reported that the only way to see us would be from a crow's nest.

Eddie and I turned the clothes and blankets as they dried and prepared a snack. Four potatoes were ready in the ashes. We opened a tin of sardines, took two potatoes, mashed them all together, cut the other two in half and made it into four portions. A hot brew of tea and a handful of wild cress, which I found down in a hollow at the burnside, made a very good little bite. The heat from the fire and a thin cigarette made us sleepy and all four of us soon dozed off.

When we wakened, the rain had stopped and the fire was dead, but all our blankets and clothes were dry. Careful packing and clearing up was the order of the day and we were anxious to start our walk.

We calculated that we were about fifteen miles from the Swiss border, and that it would not take long to reach it. We took one last look around. I picked up two of the firestones and took them down to the side of the stream. As I turned to come back, I immediately sensed that something was wrong. Percy and Eddie were standing with hands up. Henry, a few paces away, was standing to attention. At his side there was a woodsman in green and he had his gun within a foot of Henry's ear. Eddie spoke quietly.

'Don't make any move to run away or towards Joe here, or he will shoot Henry.'

With hands up I came towards the group. As I passed Henry, I looked at the woodsman and smiled and said, 'Good morning.' Then I turned to Eddie who was probably the best German speaker and said, 'Ask him if we can lower our arms and sit down – say we have no guns.' The woodsman thought for a minute, then nodded and said, 'I am a very good shot. See.' He stepped back, looked up into the trees and pointed to a pigeon high up. Without really sighting, he raised his gun, fired, and the bird came tumbling down to land about ten yards away. He walked over to it, picked it up, but before putting it into his bag he showed us a clean hole through the pigeon's head. We all nodded silently. We understood what he meant.

For half an hour we sat and talked. We told him who we were, where we were going, but now our plans were in his hands to do with as he wished. We would go back to Hohenfels if he would guide us and we would not wish to run away or harm him! He patted his gun and smiled grimly at this, stood up and said, 'Come'. We collected our gear and he pointed down the hillside through a break in the trees. We set off in single file. After half a mile or so, we came to a well-built hut. He had a key and opened the door, motioned us to sit down and spoke on a telephone just inside the door. On finishing, he locked the door, pointed along the track to the river and held up two fingers and muttered something like 'kilometres.' We were on our way again.

Round a long swinging bend we could see the towers and turrets of a castle and it was obvious we were making in that direction. Sooner than we expected, we arrived at the castle. A caretaker in green met us and led us down steps, opened a heavy door and motioned us in. He then closed the door, leaving us to survey our new quarters. We were in a large rectangular room with narrow windows starting at eight feet and rising about twenty feet. The light from these windows enabled us to see. Round two sides were stone seats with mattresses, two very strong tables and six chairs. The ceiling and cornice were decorated and painted, and two walls were heavily panelled. Percy sat down, looked around and said, 'Not much chance of getting out of here in a hurry.'

Henry looked him in the eye and put his finger to his lips.. We had got out of the way of looking for bugs in a new room. Not until we had been in for some time would we speak openly, although we did not think there would be anything in such a place as this room. Eddie produced an old pack of cards. 'We rolled a cigarette and settled down to a game, trying to be as casual as if we did not care too much. Sitting at the table-end looking towards the door, I noticed a slight movement. I was knocked out in the first game at three all and so had time to watch the door. There was another movement, a small panel was slid aside and then closed. Henry won the first game and as we were shuffling for our next round, I told them very quietly not to look at the door because we were being watched. We played for about an hour, then, packed it in. Eddie sat down to a game of Patience: we three moved nearer the door passing pointed remarks. 'Could do with a drink,' said one of us. 'Wonder when lunch is served?' asked another. 'Bacon and egg would be nice,' joined in a third, and so on, but it made no difference.

Another hour slowly went past and then we heard a quiet knock on the door. In came the uniformed caretaker. He spoke in German but when we showed that we did not fully understand, he spoke in English, making it clear that his English was probably better than our German. He explained that he had been in touch with Hohenfels and that a guard would be sent in three or four days to take us back. Meanwhile, we could stay in the quarters we were in, or we could move upstairs into a better room so long as we gave our word that we would not try to escape, nor damage the building. The railway line had been bombed and there was a new section of troops in the area. With little or no discussion, we agreed to move upstairs. It was a better-furnished room, part of a library, and we would be there until a guard arrived. The room had two double bunk beds and there was a room off it for toilet and washing which was, as Percy remarked, 'just like home'. I will not repeat our response to this quip!

Chapter 17

Honour Bound

Four bowls of soup and a sandwich with sausage were brought in and laid out on the table. We had not had anything like this for almost three years. We were very grateful and gave the keeper a packet of tea and half a tin of coffee. He went out and brought in his wife who appeared very grateful and was profuse in her thanks.

The following morning, a Feltwebel and a guard arrived from Stalag 383. They both lived in the Munich area and had come by lorry, but would have to wait until the railway was re-opened before returning. This was a calculated break for them and if we behaved they could go and visit their girlfriends! If we did not agree, we would be put into that rotten police prison. We agreed, and everyone was pleased. The guards went off saying that one of them would come each day to see us.

We were left on our own. Later, the caretaker and his wife must have had a little head-to-head talk about us. They obviously were used to having visitors to take around the castle and said that they would show us some of the rooms, but not all. They were not accustomed to war and did not agree with what was happening. We were shown some rooms; there was much of interest and we were sorry when our tour was finished. When I asked if there were any drawing materials to draw my friends, I was given some old calendars, white on the back, and a pencil, and spent the afternoon sketching my three models. When the caretaker saw them he asked if I would draw his daughter. This was the first intimation that there was a girl in the castle. While the others nodded, I said I would have to see her first. The caretaker went out to return almost immediately with mother and daughter, a girl of around nine or ten. She was very beautiful.

The reaction in the room was electric. All four of us stood up, struck dumb. This situation was completely different to anything we had previously encountered and we did not know how to cope. For four or five years we had experienced war and imprisonment and all it meant and here we were faced with an entirely different situation. We were shattered. The three who had come in hand-in-hand just stood looking at us for a full minute, then the man spoke quietly.

'This is Beate, my daughter, and we'd like you to draw her.'

I felt three pairs of eyes looking straight in my direction and nodding. I looked back and slowly shook my head. I did not know the girl; I felt I could put lines and marks on paper, but it would not be this little girl. Again I shook my head. The mother took a step forward and from behind her back produced three or four sheets of paper and three new pencils.

'Try,' she said, 'Please try.'

As I stood irresolute I had a flashback to Art College. I was in Life Room Two on a Wednesday morning for a life drawing session. Everybody was working, changing angles and rubbing out and Penny B, our tutor, was standing slightly behind me. In front was Vic Mancini, our male model, and we were to draw his head and shoulders.

'You'll have to feel the planes better,' she said. 'Half close your eyes and keep on trying. Take a fresh paper and try and try. It'll come.'

I jerked back. Here I was, five years later and another lady was saying, 'Try'. I gave a brief nod of assent. Everyone relaxed a little and began the talk. The father appeared with two chairs and set them down where the light was coming in from one of the high windows and Beate sat down and looked at me. For an hour I sat and took measurements and made some preliminary sketches. I tried various backgrounds and used different poses, and then a mug of tea was brought in. I gave Percy a pencil and he used some of the old calendars to see what he could do. Then Henry joined in drawing Eddie, and so we proceeded with an art lesson with me putting down my pencil from time to time and giving some instruction. It was good to be creative once again.

All this time the little girl sat and looked in different directions, changing around to suit me. The others moved their seats to suit themselves. At one point when her mother returned (the parents having gone out and left her with us) she asked for a doll to be brought and she sat and played gently with it, singing little songs and nursery rhymes. And so it was, and I was getting nowhere! Finally I said, 'We'll try again tomorrow morning.' The others were quite pleased with what I had done, perhaps a bit over-critical, but I did not object to this. Eddie said, 'Not bad!' And I took this as high praise. The mother said she had found more paper, some tinted, and a light brown pencil.

I was up early the following morning to wander around and absorb the atmosphere of the place. I finished up in the music room where there was a small piano. Opening the lid, I began picking out some little Scottish airs. One kept repeating itself to me; it was 'The Lea Rig'.

> 'When ower the hill the evening star,
> Tells buchtin' time is near, my jo,
> I'll meet thee on the lea-rig,
> My ain kind dearie, O.'

Having played it once or twice I felt a little bump and there was my little model wishing to play. She sat down, put her fingers on the keys and began. I was amazed. This was the girl I was to draw and I was now seeing her for the first time. She played on for some moments and then began to sing in a little voice that was quite enchanting. I was desperate to begin my drawing when her mother came in to say that breakfast was ready. A plate of porridge, a cup of tea and a slice of bread were more than enough and I was preparing my papers and pencils and itching to begin.

About two hours later I put down my pencils, gathered up the sketches and spare paper and said to Beate, 'That's it finished. I'm going for a short walk.' I looked down at my effort. It was probably the best drawing I had ever done. Completely drained, I finished off my cold tea and went out. When I came back, mother, daughter and my three were standing round the table-end looking at my drawing, almost afraid to touch it. I picked it up and leaned it against a board at an angle, stood back and asked, 'Will that do?' Not a word was spoken. They were looking at the drawing, then at me, then back to the drawing. When I looked at the mother, she bent down, picked up her daughter and I saw that she had tears running down her cheeks. Eddie was the first to speak.

'You're not to cry! We are very pleased and happy too. And we're not crying.'

The sergeant from Stalag 383 arrived at midday. There would not be a train on that line until the next day. We would stay where we were for another night and he would go and see his girlfriend. He and the other two guards would come at one o'clock in time to catch the train. In the meantime, he would take us for a walk to see his river: he was a keen fisherman. He gave the mother a receipt for us. We left our gear and set out. An hour's walk and we slowed down. The scenery was lovely. He showed us the Blenheim battlefield of 1704 when the river was red with blood. We turned a corner and there was the river. This was the Isar. When I heard the name I quoted from *Hohenlinden*:

> *'On Linden, when the sun was low,*
> *All bloodless lay the untrodden snow,*

And dark as winter was the flow
Of Isar, rolling rapidly.'

We sat down and had a smoke. The guard kept talking about a present for his girlfriend. Two yards out in the water, with smaller stones to the bank, there was a long flat stone. I slipped off my jacket and rolled up the right sleeve of my shirt and lay down along the stone. When I was comfortable I dropped my arm into the current. It was pleasantly warm. A minute or two and I felt that wonderful excitement and thrill that runs through the body when a fish slides into the hand. It was only a small one, but it was an indication that fish used that route. Five more minutes or thereabouts and I felt myself go rigid; there was a fish to hand. I knew I had to relax and so I began to tickle it with my pinkie. Against the slow current it turned over on its side so I kept my little finger moving gently while sliding my hand along the body until my finger and thumb were just touching the gills. The whole of my body was set. I did a half-roll, whipped my hand out of the water and landed a fish at the feet of the four on the bank. They were absolutely stunned.

I stepped over beside them. Percy was looking for a stone to knap the fish, so I picked it up by the tail, ran my hand along to the gills, straightened it out, turned it upside down and tapped it sharply on the toe of my boot. One convulsive move from the fish and I laid it at the feet of the sergeant.

'A present for your *fräulein*,' I said with a smile.

It was a beauty: a pound and a half of silver scales and pink spots. I took out my knife with the broken small blade, made a hole through the gills and looped a length of string so that it would easily be carried. We could not get back quickly enough. When we arrived at the castle, the good lady fetched a sheet of white paper, put it into a narrow basket and laid the fish in a bed of parsley and mint.

'Thank you, thank you all round, I will see you tomorrow,' and the sergeant was away with his present.

We sat down and had a game of Bridge. When the keeper came in he was taken to see my drawing. He stood as the others had done, not speaking for a full two minutes, then said something quietly to his wife. The next morning he came to us.

'You gave your word and you have kept it, but I want you to go further and promise me that you will never speak of my secret if I should tell it.'

We stood bewildered.

'We cannot give our word,' I said, 'for anything that does not affect ourselves. We will never speak of you or the way you have treated us until after the war and then it will only be to show our appreciation and thanks.'

He held up his hand and stopped me speaking. After a supper of soup and potatoes we went off to sleep wondering what the secret was to be.

After breakfast, we were taken downstairs to a long cellar. The mother was waiting. She came up to me, put her finger to her lips, nodding, and I nodded back. Then she moved on to Eddie, then Percy and Henry. A massive door was opened and we were taken inside. There was a strong wooden frame slotted top and bottom, and in between were pictures of various sizes. The caretaker began to show them to us, one at a time. He would unlock one, show it, replace it and lock it in once more. For the others, this was a show of very beautiful pictures, but I soon realised that I was viewing some of the most valuable works of art from various countries of Europe. In two years at the College of Art, I had seen books and prints in libraries, but here I was looking at original paintings of very great value. I could have spent weeks in a place like this, but time was up and an indication was made to go out. When we reached the upstairs room I said, 'Thank you for allowing us to see what we have just seen.'

'These are not mine,' he replied, 'they belong to Herr Göring and must not be spoken of until after the war is over. If it was known outside this building, Beate, my wife and I would be shot.' Then he added, 'The drawing you drew of my little girl is more precious than all these put together.'

The sergeant and his two privates arrived in time to catch a train to Augsburg. All the formalities and cancellation of promises were written down and we said goodbye to our captors. The guards set their guns and we were told, 'If one runs away, one of your friends will be shot.' We were back on the old footing and we nodded in understanding. Beate and her mother were both crying when we marched away out of the gate. From Augsburg we took a second-class carriage to Ulm and from there we were put into a wagon with one guard until we arrived near Hohenfels. We were the last of the escapees from the potato fields to return.

Back to the guardroom we were taken, where, fortunately, there was a complete new set of guards, and then to the Commandant for a very long interrogation. He could not understand why we tried to escape. He had a good camp and we should settle down and enjoy the peace and quiet. The interviews ceased abruptly when I asked the interpreter to enquire of the Commandant what he would be doing if our positions were reversed. He sat for a full two minutes without speaking and then he said, 'Thirty days in Straflager for all four,' and we were taken away.

There was a shortage of food in Germany at this time. Red Cross parcels were being held up 'because of the bombing' and so thirty days on bread and water was hard to bear. We just lay on our beds and waited for soup days, every third day, to come and so time passed very slowly. We were allowed to walk round the prison square for an hour each day but not allowed to communicate with our friends across the road. Sometimes there were books to read, especially for those who were studying and there were New Testaments in every second cell. Mail was very erratic and then one day after a fortnight or so we each received a bundle of anything between eight to fifteen letters. These were read very slowly and every now and then somebody would shout, 'Listen to this … ' and we would hear another story. Time then passed quickly and we were soon returning to our old quarters. The day we were marched into camp, I said to the others, 'Well, that's the end of our break. I'm sorry I didn't go further.'

All three stopped and agreed.

'We wouldn't have missed it for anything. Let us know when the next one's to be.'

Rations and handcuffs

The penalty for being without cuffs: one hour in the sun with hands up

The author does not know the full story behind this photograph but it appears that four German airmen who were shot down in the North Sea managed to drift in a dingy to the French coast where the Germans picked them up. Apparently, their hands were tied. The reprisal for this came in an order from German HQ to handcuff a number of prisoners of war for a week, and accordingly, a fully armed company of guards marched into camp putting cuffs on seventy prisoners. They stated that they would return to unlock them in the evening.

Bert Smiles from the author's hut was a professional burglar in Civvy Street. Following careful instructions from Bert, the author drew a sketch of the inside of a handcuff, then, with a piece of strong wire cut from a fence, he made a key. It worked! Within half an hour the author had visited tea huts and had unlocked seven sets of cuffs which were then hung behind the door to be picked up later. The penalty for being without cuffs was one hour in the sun with hands up. The Germans soon tired of the exercise and the whole farce was abandoned within a week.

Chapter 18

Bankau-Luft 7

Back in Stalag 383, I settled down to make preparations for a further 'walk'. Despite the drop in food supplies, I wanted to be fit should an occasion arise. A run in food parcels for three weeks was a great help. And then there came the warning: 'Escaping is no longer a sport. Prisoners caught trying to escape would be shot.' This was a blow. It meant, of course, that any thought of escaping would have to be a certain, secure plan, and we were aware that getting into Basel or any part of Switzerland would be very difficult. The shortage of food was a definite factor in making the Germans edgy, and there were too many of them ready to shoot at the slightest excuse. Then news filtered through that forty or fifty men from Sagan who escaped were lined up at the roadside to stretch their legs and have a pee and had been murdered where they stood, their bodies cremated to hide the evidence. At Hohenfels, we believed at first that this was all propaganda, but when stories persisted, we had to give it serious thought.

Added to this was the feeling that the end was not far away. After four years of suffering, it would be a pity to be shot when freedom was near and yet there was with me the yearning to be back on the moor, to meet freely with people, to laugh and talk and go where I wished with no thought of a gun at my back, or dead bodies lying in woods or at the roadsides, and no more scratching around for tobacco, dried roots or weeds to smoke to try and quell the awful gnawing hunger that was slowly killing many of my comrades. The uncertainty of everything was very stressful and did not help amicable relationships. However, walking slowly round the perimeter wire, we decided that it was ninety-to-ten in favour of staying in Stalag 383 until we were released. And then the Germans announced that all RAF prisoners were to be moved away to a new camp in eastern Germany near the Polish frontier.

Why? Were we to act as hostages to the advancing Russian army? Was there not enough food in the west? This new camp was to hold over one thousand men. Into the picture came Baronowski and one or two other Polish airmen who were with us. Baron's parents lived about forty miles from the new camp and he knew the countryside well. He would show us everything when we got there – unless the Germans molested his folks. Knowing that we would be searched going out as well as coming in, all the hiding cunning came into play. We would need our forging papers. As Baron assured us that he would manage to have the local workers' permits sent in, and also inks, pens, and paper, we had no need to worry about too much. If we could get out of the new camp (we had not seen it yet) there would be contacts to look after us. An important factor was the food situation. Trains were running eastwards with food for the German troops and so it might just be possible for Red Cross parcels to get through as well. All of this was sheer speculation which only highlighted our impatience.

We were herded into trucks with no food or water. To begin with, we thought it was going to be a short journey, but twenty-four hours later we were shunted into a siding and allowed out for toilet and a drink. A ring of guards with cocked rifles surrounded us and stood stolidly looking at us. An hour later another truck was brought up alongside with bread, water and everyone received a ladle of soup in a dixie. The sceptics went to town when this was dished up. 'We must be going on to China with all this,' they said sarcastically.

Inmates of Hut 117: author, centre front. Back row: Baronowski, second from left; Pete, second from right. *The inmates of Hut 117 were all special prisoners: escapees. There had been forty odd escapes from this group. (Photo taken with a smuggled camera.)*

Back in the trucks, we sat and waited. The railway lines were busy all along the Danube valley, but we finally chugged our way to a side line which took us to a siding where we were allowed out to face the usual row of guns and told to form up in fives. Once more we were warned: if anyone tries to escape, one of his friends will be shot. We marched off until we came to the familiar watchtowers and barbed wire. And thus it was that we arrived at Bankau-Luft 7 in October 1944.

Airmen from all over Germany were being drafted in. They brought with them a wealth of experience from a variety of camps and came with the determination to work on as many good ideas as possible. Many of the new men were still having wounds dressed, but they also brought in the latest news and songs. We still did not fully understand the reason for the move and settled down to make the best of it. Walking round the trip wire one day, I met up with Baronowski. Baron was a bit worried about his mother and father and desperately wanted to see them. He had been warned in Stalag 8B and Stalag 383 that if he tried to escape, his parents could be shot or taken off to work as foreign workers somewhere in Germany. His sister was away from home and Baron had a note from her to the effect that she was well and was working in a laundry *'somewhere in G'* and hoped to see him soon. Baron was a Spitfire pilot who had come down in the Channel and had found himself in his rubber dinghy. He once told us his own story: 'I sit on the water. Water is all I see. I listen. What do I hear? A *ploop, ploop*. I move my foot. A hole in the boat! I put my finger in the hole ... water stops. Then I think, what if little fish come and bite my finger? Then boat comes and here I am.'

There was no doubt Baron was troubled. He did not wish to involve others in an attempt to escape, and yet initially he needed help. Finally, he blurted out, 'You cover if I go?'

I took his hand and gave it a shake. 'Yes, I'll help you if at all possible.'

'You cut wire?'

I nodded. That was enough: we went ahead with plans. After a walk or two round the wire, we decided to 'go' at a corner where two wire poles were only two yards apart. This meant that the position of the watchtower lights threw a heavy shadow under the double wire lasting for forty-seven seconds before swinging away and then coming back. The foot guards trudged back and forward and sometimes stopped to have a smoke and a chat. For two weeks we timed every move after darkness fell and lights came on until we had a good record of timing. This settled, we got two long lengths of string, blackened them, and had them ready. Pete and Henry volunteered to sit in the shadow of a hut and signal us when guards were approaching.

Baron was travelling light: he reckoned he would be in touch with friends within two miles. He went first, straight across into a dark shadow, flat out with wire cutters, and a dark green ground sheet pulled up over. I followed at the next light swing with cutters and some loose ends of barbed wire. Straight over and I dived under the sheet and we both started cutting. It took a long time because the wire was double twisted at the corner, but we made steady progress with only one interruption. Then, just as Baron reached the outside wire, we received a signal to stop. Coming along the path was a soldier with a large Alsatian dog at his side. When he came to the watchtower he shouted up to the guard. By good fortune for us, it was a pal and they started to chat. Meanwhile, the dog came over to the fence, lifted his leg, and then started to sniff along until he was about a foot from Baron's face. The first I knew of this was when Baron went rigid. I was lying half across him, holding a wire that was threatening to spring away. Then I heard, 'Good dog ... good dog.' It struck me as being funny. Here was a Pole, whispering loudly and in English to a German dog and I started a shaking laugh. At this point one of the camp rabbits made a run to the bushes over the roadway. With a loud bark, the dog started after it, and with a louder shout, the keeper started after the dog. Baron cut the last wire and then paused. 'You bloody haggis! You laugh. See you later,' and he was off.

I twisted the outside wires together and with all eyes on the bushes where dog and man were thrashing around, managed to reverse out into a shadow, tying up and mending the hole. By the time the guard came along, I had caught the ground sheet and I edged round the thicker pole until he had passed. I gathered up the cutters and odd bits of wire and started counting the seconds until the lights met and parted. I was briefly back at Lanark on sports day, Jimmy Mitchell at the starting line. 'On your marks; get set,' and before he could say, 'Go', I was off. But there was no re-call this time. With one foot pressing the pole I was off and did that twenty-five yards in even time. Next, I was over the trip wire and back into the hut.

I handed over the gear to the escapee member just in case the hut should be searched because it was close to the main wire. We set up a cover for morning parade and kept it going for a week, one man from one end slipping along to the other end. On the third day, a worker who was uplifting vegetable rubbish from the cookhouse dropped a note which was picked up. All it said was, *'Ol OK B.'* We knew then that Baron had made a home run. Some three weeks later, a woman worker passed on the news that the family of Baronowski had moved away to live with relatives near Warsaw, and that the son was going to Britain to fly in aeroplanes!

Weeks passed into months and at last long-awaited mail began to arrive from home. As the camp was in a very dull area near the Polish Border I think the guards believed they would be amongst the first to be taken if the Russians advanced quickly and they did not know what to do. Food was now down to minimum rations, and bones were beginning to show where they had not shown before. Then came the command: we were to be marched out into Germany. We were to take part in the Master Plan. Troops from all fronts were to mass in companies around Berlin and, at a given signal, they would burst out and annihilate all the enemies of the Reich. Prisoners were to be used as workers or hostages where contact was made before the drive out.

On 19th January 1945 we were set to leave Bankau-Luft 7 behind.

Chapter 19

Escape to Poland

O n the morning of the march, two of our recent prisoners died. In a
small cemetery at the end of the camp, they were duly buried.
This gave Pete and I an idea. Two extra graves were dug! Such
was the shambles generally around us, with the wounded being
carried to over-loaded wagons and the walking wounded being helped to
the parade for counting, that we were able to slip our gear into the graves,
slide in ourselves, were covered, and the grass sod carefully laid on top.
Two small pipes at one end and loose holes gave us air. Henry, in charge
of the job, stamped around and told us that the marks could scarcely be
seen. He wished us luck and said he hoped to get the march started as
soon as possible.

It was cold lying in one position. This was something we had not
practised, nor had we had time to line our hole with straw or hay or spruce
branches and although we were below the frost level, the temperature was
very low. I realised that we would probably have to crawl out sooner than
we thought. Then we heard voices and doors banging: three or four guards

were opening doors and looking into huts, then closing them before passing on. Footsteps passed over us. The door of the gravedigger's hut was opened and closed; a voice shouted *'Alles'* and then there was quietness. The guards were in no mood to hang around and they were off to join the tail of the column that was slowly heading away from the camp.

With a great effort, I pushed up the sod and looked at the sky. There was no feeling in my fingers and I wondered if I had frostbite, but no! A further stiff movement and I eased my cold body out into the warm air. There was no movement from Pete. He was lying with closed eyes and for a moment I thought he was sleeping. I gave him a shake. 'Breakfast up,' I said and then realised that he was like a log, frozen stiff. With frantic pushing and pulling, I rolled him over the grass until he started to move by himself. We grasped hands and raised and lowered, and out and in, until we began to come back to normal. Then we worked on knees and feet, stamping and bending until our whole bodies began to unfreeze.

'We're mad,' I said, 'just plain mad.'

'True,' said Pete, 'but we're free, free, free,' and he began to dance around, and I joined in, round a hut and back again.

'Right, we'll gather up and go down to the cook house – it'll be warm in there.'

The temperature in the cookhouse was high compared to the outside. In one corner there was a boiler that had not been completely emptied. We had a long warm drink, then steeped our hands in warm water and raised our temperature by quite a few degrees until we were back to normal. Looking around the place, we found some overalls and tried them on, and finally found a pair to fit reasonably well. We decided to take them with us so that we could pretend we were workmen; they would also help to keep out the cold.

We agreed to put some miles between the camp and us. On the south side we struck a road and walked along for about three miles before we came to some houses. All the old precautions that we had previously used returned to us. An empty house across the road had a low hedge. We jumped over into the garden and hid down to watch the goings-on in the other houses. Everything appeared normal with no green uniforms or rifles. A workman came down the road on a bicycle, leaned it against the wall and went into the house across the road. Then two girls came along; they chatted for a minute and one went on to a house further down, the other into the first house.

'Let's ask for a drink of water,' said Pete.

We were not a very presentable pair, with overalls that were stained and badly fitting, but we crossed the road and knocked. A lady I took to be the wife of the man who had gone in earlier opened the door. Pete tried his German. I tried my French. Pete tried some English. The only response was a quiet shake of the head. Then Pete produced his flask, turned it upside down to show it was empty and held it out. Again there was hesitation. In a quiet voice I said, 'Baronowski'. The result was startling. The woman turned and shouted something into the room; the man and girl came rushing to the door, stood looking for ten seconds, then grabbed us and pulled us into the room. The door was shut, two wooden chairs appeared and we were made to sit down. A drink was produced without asking and then the introductions and questions began. The first thing we did was to slip off the overalls. When the mud-marked uniform was seen, there was a great understanding. I indicated that I wanted a piece of paper, produced a pencil, and when a scribble pad was placed before me, I drew a rough sketch of the empty camp with open gates and a column of men marching away. There was a clapping of hands. Then the lady took away our tunics. Two large shirts were laid out with two pairs of baggy trousers beside them. We were directed into a washroom and handed a razor and signs made to use them. A tiny white-haired lady came in and we were given a full explanation as she spoke English. The two girls worked in a small laundry. Our clothes were taken away for the evening shift and returned three hours later, cleaned and ironed. When we had changed, brushed our hair and shaved, they stood us up and approved. The old lady said we were now ready to travel and all we needed was food and more food. Before she went away she said, 'I will bring back friends to see you.'

We stayed with this family for three or four days. We met many friends and neighbours brought food for ourselves and the family who were distantly related to Baron. Two young men came in to say that they would bring Polish papers and would take us to Warsaw where we could decide whether to go on to Odessa or north to the Baltic where we would find a Swedish boat to smuggle us towards Britain. A long, very fond farewell, with the promise to try and return some day, and we were away.

Chapter 20

South from Warsaw

The journey to Warsaw was uneventful but we began to see more green uniforms. Papers were looked at whenever any suspicious characters like us were seen moving about. In Warsaw, we were picked up by two fourteen year-old boys, guided down a side street, and then down steps into a large chamber leading to the main sewer.

'Stay here with this family for a day or two until we find a safe train. We'll also find out other routes. Go to sleep because we may have to travel by night.'

These were our instructions. At night the place emptied but all returned in the morning with food and information. Odessa was a very doubtful destination as there were many troops returning to Germany and wagons and food trains were piling up on the rails. At this early stage of the retreat, the roads had long queues of refugees making their way to what they believed to be safety. A new route was mentioned which we were willing to consider and which involved finding friends in a small boat sailing north to the Baltic Sea on the Oder. From Riga we would have to get in touch with a friendly Swedish captain. Europe was opening up for us, but with distances of three to seven hundred miles from which to choose, life became like the whole of that country, very difficult and, indeed, a shambles.

Two railway workers got in touch with us. They were loading wagons with food crates and knew those that were to go to the German troops and others that were going direct to Odessa. There were some very good officials to whom we would be introduced in the main station at Odessa and from there we would be escorted to a direct route through to Great Britain. We decided to try Odessa and set off following the two wagon loaders. They led us along a railway yard and pointed out the two lines of wagons – one for Odessa and one for the front. We had just reached the wagon into which we were to go when round the engine came six or seven Germans checking both lines. We were given a crate each and motioned into a wagon nearest to where we stood. Placing the crates along the half-open doorway we hid down in a corner. One of the workers pointed to his wrist, put up one finger, then pointed to himself to indicate that he would come back and open the door. We gave him the thumbs-up sign and settled down.

Along came the guards, checking that all wagons were full. Our door was closed and we heard the snib going in, then quietness. We shifted boxes and crates around and gave ourselves some room and stretched our legs to await the coming of our friend. A blowing of whistles, a shout, and we began to slip forward! We were instantly on our feet: we were in the wrong train. We were on a troop train for the eastern front and we did not wish to go there! Then it slowed down, the engine was uncoupled and it moved away. Three hundred yards it went, then, it shunted back and picked up our row of wagons and slowly moved them away on to another line. The engine returned, coupled up and we started to move out; it was obviously on its way to Odessa.

Long past the panic stage, we sat down to examine our position.

We would have to try to open the door so that we could slip out when it suited us. To that end we tackled a crate that was slightly burst, managed to tear off a spar and loosen a wire. The crate was filled with *Knakebrot*, rolled out sheets of wheat and rye, which were very palatable with water or soup. We squeezed out a sheet, broke it into pieces, nibbled away for half an hour, then filled our big pockets with enough to keep us going for three or four days.

The wire that was round the crates was quite soft, and so we twisted two lengths to strengthen it and fashioned a hook at one end. Although we could not see the sneck, we had a feeling that we could slide the wire through a hole and 'fish' with the hook for a ring that would lift the bar. Half an hour each, with frozen fingers and no success, we had to admit defeat. We sat down on the burst crate and worked out that if only one man were to open the door, we would place two crates close up and push them out on top of him, hoping that, in the confusion, we could drop down and hide under the wagon.

All this time we were sweeping along at a fair speed. The countryside, or what we could see of it, was white and it was snowing steadily. Sitting in our corner, becoming drowsy, I was looking across at the other side when I noticed a side panel moving slightly from the vertical line of a pile of crates. I jumped up and began shifting boxes and crates until I reached the opposite side of the wagon. There was a movable bar on the floor. We both stood on it and when it went down, we grasped a long handle and pulled. A door slid open and there we were gazing out into the open countryside. This was the side for heavy goods and horses. We prepared our exit as we had done before so that we could slip out either side if necessary. About two hours later, we ran slowly through a large goods yard and stopped just outside a huge hangar. There were men in all kinds of dress everywhere (we would not have looked out of place in our overalls) but we hung back and waited. Three wagons were uncoupled and we moved away. A half a mile past houses, the engine turned along a sidetrack and came to a stop. One man was left to look after the engine and all the others went off to a well-lit building behind a waiting room.

We got down and went back along the line, having noticed a farm building and cottage as we were coming in. When we reached it, we listened. There was no dog barking which meant that the farmer and his family had gone. We crawled into a hay barn, snuggled deep into the hay and went to sleep. Waking early into a cold, white day, we started walking as soon as possible to get away from the populated area. After a steady march, we saw what we wanted: a long row of tanks, lorries, and extra transport heading westwards. Watching it from half a mile away, we saw it come to a halt. Five minutes later, we advanced towards the nearest tank, raised our hands and shouted. A small jeep-type car came round the tank, stopped beside us and two dressed officers spoke. We shrugged and shook our heads. We tried French, German and then I said, 'We are English' in my best Scottish accent. One of the officers went to tank three and the tank commander came down, spoke in perfect English and asked how we came to be there. We told him.

'How far to the food wagons?' he asked.

We told him everything and every word was translated. Four tanks set off, taking us as guides.

By nine o'clock, the tanks were at the siding, two on either side.

'Where are the guards?' we were asked.

We pointed to the wagon nearest the engine which immediately received a burst of machine gun fire followed by a lorry with twenty Russian soldiers driving up and taking over. The four tanks wheeled round and went to rejoin the main unit. We joined the two officers in the jeep and were told that we would probably go ahead of the tanks and inform British working parties to stay in their camps until the second line troops from Russia released them.

Russian prisoners: *as Russia was not a member of the Geneva Convention, prisoners in Germany did not receive Red Cross Food Parcels nor help with food and clothing from home. Their condition as they waited for their troops to arrive, despite a little help from other prisoners, is evident in these two photos.*

Chapter 21

Burns' Night on the Oder

On and on we went, allowing nothing to hinder the drive to Berlin. Two days later, the only large obstacle on our way was the River Oder which was partly frozen over in places, with many of the bridges mined. The weather was atrocious; an inch of snow on one side of our coats helped to keep us warm, but still it came, almost horizontally, driven by a very strong wind. We reached the river and drove into a large State farm where six tanks took up places on the open side, facing outwards, ready to move. We were inside a large courtyard with out-houses on each side for vehicles and storage for hay and straw. We slipped into a corner in the section of straw and booked a bed. Fires were being lit all round the open yard and clothes and coats were hung up on makeshift hangers to unfreeze and dry out. A large boiler of very thick soup arrived and we were allowed to fill up dixies. This was indeed very satisfying. We settled back in the straw, a bit drowsy and then a voice, a girl's voice was heard.

'Where is the Scotsman?'

I felt the hair at my neck rising, and wondered, 'What next?' I struggled to my feet, and there she stood, second-in-command of a Russian Women's Tank Unit, a round muff hat on her head and looking very neat and official in a dark green uniform. She addressed me directly.

'Do you know what week this is?'

Just a little bewildered, I shook my head.

'This is Robert Burns' week, and tonight you will recite his poetry and sing his songs. I will translate for all these people.'

My mind flashed back to my primary school. I was, for the first time, thankful that 'old Cooke', the headmaster there, had driven me by fear of his tawse to learn and sing Burns' works.

'I do not know,' I started to say, but was stopped by an imperious wave of a hand.

'All my relations in Scotland can recite and sing our national Bard – where do you begin?'

Between twenty and thirty had gathered round our fire, and were told, 'Andrew from Scotland will entertain.' I took a step forward, dropped on to one knee, scraped around as if I was catching something, picked up a handful of hay and stood up smoothing it in my hand into a small ball and started.

> *'Wee, sleekit, courin' tim'rous beastie,*
> *O, whit a panic's in thy breastie.'*

I stopped, and the girl translated, and so I carried on, one line or two at a time. I missed out a verse here and there, but finished the last two:

> *'But mousie, thou are no' thy lane,*
> *In proving foresight may be vain,*
> *The best laid schemes o' mice and men*
> *Gang aft agley.'*

The reception shook me. There was clapping and smiling and nodding: a complete understanding, and so I gave them *'To a Daisy'*. Next, the girl did some explaining before a cook came in with a large sausage. I addressed the 'haggis', cut it into slices. Many came up, took a slice and went back and sat down facing me – they obviously wished for more. I walked round the front row, stopped beside a fair-haired girl, put out my hand and asked her to come forward. She assented (without knowing what was wanted) and we walked back to my stance. We turned round. I nodded to my interpreter, and began:

> *'O, my luve is like a red, red rose,*
> *That's newly sprung in June.'*

Line for line I said it, and slowly walked her back to where she had sat and then, in a very quiet voice I began to sing.

> *'And fare thee weel, my only luve,*
> *And fare thee weel, a while!*
> *And I will come again, my luve,*
> *Tho' it were ten thousand mile.'*

Well, the applause was terrific. If this is what they want, I'll be here all night, I thought. I'd better give them something else, and so I began again with the translation continuing until the last verse.

> *Is there for honest poverty*
> *'For a' that, an a' that,*
> *That man to man the world o'er,*
> *Shall brithers be for a' that.'*

Everybody stood up, shaking hands. Given a signal, they all sat down.

'I will sing a song of Robert Burns,' announced the second-in-command whose relatives had lived on the banks of Loch Ness, and who until this point had been translating the poems.

A trained voice sang out *'Ye banks and braes o' bonnie Doon'* in a language they all understood. On the second verse I joined in quietly, 'la, la, la' to the end, then she added, 'We will sing it as Burns wrote it.'

'Ye banks and braes...'

I sang the words in a low contralto, as I had heard it sung in the Hall at home. On the second verse, she took my hand and we wandered dreamily across the front. I smelled the briar and heard the birds singing. She pulled a rose and I pretended to put it in her hair and we finished the song in unison. There was a second or two of complete silence before everyone jumped up, clapping and chattering, touching each other, moving around us and trying to shake our hands. The numbers had doubled and they were milling around and laughing with pleasure. I was completely shattered. Here was I, shut in with a group of people who had travelled hundreds of miles in tanks fitted with guns, with the sole intention of wreaking vengeance on a country that had dared to destroy them; and a freezing wind blowing snow from the Baltic ocean bringing everything to a standstill and kindly covering the dead and dying women and children lying in groups along the roadsides. And a sad little song with a Scottish air and words by Robert Burns, written two hundred years before, had changed the world around us!

I was uplifted and a bit dazed, and yes, I was proud – a sort of humble pride, pleased and delighted – and then two hands on my shoulders turned me round and my hands were taken in hers and an emotional voice spoke, 'Tonight I am your Jean: tonight you are my Robert.'

A large door at one end of the courtyard swung open. There stood our little jeep with two officers who made their way to the Commander with a message. She stood up on a chair to a table in a hushed silence. 'The barges have arrived and are ready to take us across. All vehicles to be on the west side of the river before breakfast. You have half an hour to move off.' She jumped down and touched me on the shoulder. 'You go with the guides who will lead us across. I will see you there.'

The wind had dropped, there was no snow, but it was bitterly cold. We got into our dry clothes and heavy, damp coats, gathered our gear and went out to our recce unit. Right on time, a long slow line of vehicles and tanks came stretching down to the river. A broad, snow-packed ramp led them onto the flat-bottomed barges and movement began. Five hours later, the east side of the Oder was cleared and the west side was marshalled into units to go in different directions – mostly north towards Berlin. It was known that there were at least ten divisions of German troops to the south, and so many units were deployed to hold what they could until the second line arrived.

At daybreak, some sort of order was established and everything had to stand for twenty-four hours. The troops that were freed were out ransacking small towns and villages. We were sent in our van to tell other small camps and working parties to be patient until official word came that the countryside was clear. Twenty-four hours later, some sort of plan of attack had been arranged. Some of the tanks were to scour the area; we had to go west and south. I went along to the tanks and met 'Jean' in command. She explained the manoeuvre that was to take place. I stepped back, gave a salute, put my hand into my inside pocket and gave her my small volume of *Burns' Poems and Songs*. For a moment she stood irresolute, then she opened her coat, and put the book safely away. Her face had changed from the hard, weather-beaten commander to that of a quiet, bare-foot lassie somewhere in Scotland. Then she buttoned up her coat, dried her eyes and said, 'Thank you, Andrew,' turned and walked back to her tank. I, in turn, went back to my van. We never saw each other again.

For ten to twenty miles we scoured for working parties. There were German troops around and several times we had to turn back from bullets fired from cover. The countryside was a shambles; small villages and towns were overcrowded or empty. We decided that we were where we did not want to be. We were mixed into front line fighting and hiding, and looking for something to eat, and then as we entered a small town our van was hit and the driver killed. The other officer joined up with a second unit that came along. We crawled down into a cellar in a farm and decided to remain there until relieving forces were nearer.

'Jean', Second-in-Command of the Russian Tank Crew who organised the Burns' Night Celebration

'Jean' had been brought up steeped in the poetry and songs of Robert Burns as her family had lived for a time on the shores of Loch Ness. The photograph above was taken some five or six days after the author celebrated Burns' Night with Russian troops, Jean interpreting, line by line, poems recited by the author for the troops. The author received the photograph when the guards left Luckenwelde.

Chapter 22

Luckenwelde

Three days later, Peter hurried in with the news that a very long column of prisoners was being marched along the road. There were very few guards, but it was obviously heading for a railway station or a camp where there would be organised food of some kind. We slid out from the roadside and joined in with the slow walking column. Rumours were rife. We were going to an army camp where 'all fit men' would be issued with a rifle to help fight the advancing Russians. One prisoner voiced the general opinion that 'There's going to be a great number of unfit men around!' The temperature was rising steadily. Snow was melting; there were runnels of water everywhere. Homemade sledges were thrown aside and everyone was back to carrying gear.

We arrived at Pransnitz on Thursday 1st February where, we were told, we would stay for two days. 'The second day will also be a rest and then there will probably be a train and more food.' To this was added a reading of a Wehrmacht proclamation, stating that five men were to be repatriated. Who, where, when and why, were the questions asked. We had heard this story so often that no attention was paid to it. We were issued with train rations: twenty-four ounces of bread, eighteen ounces of meat, two ounces of margarine, one spoonful of sugar, two spoons of barley and two of flour and then we were marched to Goldberg. There we were packed into cattle trucks, sixty-four men in a space twenty-five feet by eight feet. We passed Leignitz at two o'clock, and arrived near Sagan at six o'clock where we were held up all night by air raids. We left Sagan at six in the morning, passed Cottbus at mid-day and reached Falkendorf at half-past two where we had our first drink of water for thirty-six hours.

Cooking a meal for four on a homemade Blower Cooker while on the march from Bankau-Luft 7

The next day was spent in a cattle truck, miserable, thirsty and hungry. We left at midnight and travelled for three hours until we arrived at Luckenwelde, detrained, and shuffled to Stalag 3A. It was Wednesday

7th February. We had been on the move in bitter winter conditions for nearly three weeks.

Stalag 3A at Luckenwelde was used by the Germans to store personal parcels that had gone astray. It also had stores of surplus cigarettes and a regular supply of food parcels. It was very well guarded and the prisoners there were placed in compounds according to nationality. The bombing and strafing of railways and other depots throughout the country had now reached such a pitch that everything had slowed down or stopped. German rations were at a very low standard, the population was hungry all the time and thousands of incomers were starving and dying.

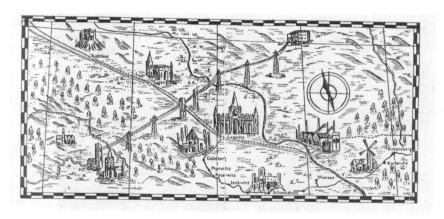

The march away from advancing Russians: map drawn by the author on his return to Art College

The map illustrates the author's state of mind as prisoners were being marched away from advancing Russians in January 1945. There were no signposts or maps – only names of small towns – and snow, ankle to knee-deep, and a great hunger for food and water.

As we were being counted going into the camp, I heard my name shouted, and there was Ned Lynch. I had not seen him since Lamsdorf days where he was in charge of organising working parties. He gave a nod, a wink and a twist of his head, turned his back and headed out towards the fringe of the crowd that was milling about awaiting instructions. I gathered Pete, Henry and Percy and followed him. When we were clear, he took us to a hut a bit to one side.

'Go into that one and settle in the corner and I'll be back with one or two more. Wait till I come,' and he was off.

Here were six two tier bunks. We took one each and got our gear all sorted out. Half an hour later, Ned came back with some friends and a small tank of tea. He also had some soup and bread. We sat down and quietly ate every crumb and drank every drop of the tea. When we finished, we said our thanks and 'now let's talk.'

And there was much to say. Ned reckoned that another two months would see the end, and therein lay the danger. The countryside swarmed with troops. The SS firmly believed that they could still win the war. The Wehrmacht, the soldiers who had marched all over the Continent singing their loud boastful songs, knew that there was only defeat ahead. Many were returning wounded, in rags, unshaven and completely demoralised. The forefront of the Russian forces was pushing forward in a race to reach Berlin before the Americans, and on their way they destroyed houses, breaking furniture to bits to make fires, taking anything they could find as souvenirs, tearing the clothes off women to look for jewellery and raping them before leaving. Shots could be heard all day long. We, in a large group, were in less danger and were warned, 'Why lose your life in the last days of the War?' The big question was – where could we find food?

Then the Red Cross parcels were issued: one parcel to two men. With cigarettes, chocolate and soap, we could barter for a few more potatoes or bread, sometimes an egg or two or a bit of sausage meat. One more load of parcels could go a long way to augment the meagre rations which were dished up daily.

Luckenwelde lay on a direct route from Berlin to the south. The Russians, after crossing the Oder, headed west and then north. The Yanks came in from the south and west and the British and French approached from the west and north. One great disadvantage was the lack of communication with our front liners. When we eventually received a wireless set, we became more impatient. During the first two weeks of April 1945, a long rugged battle took place between the Oder and Berlin. Heavy firing and much small arms firing went on day after day and then the full force of the Russian second line came in. The SS finally surrendered and were marched away.

This was the signal for all the guards. We woke up one morning to find them gone. The next day, two Russian tanks came in and cleared away about fifty yards of barbed wire but warned us to stay in camp until the whole area was freed. Then they were on their way.

The news from our wireless set was that the Americans and British troops were held up at the river Elbe. The Russians were advancing rapidly. Excitement in the camp was intense, but as far as we could make out, a major war was taking place around us. The citizens in the town banded together and fired upon Russians who were helping themselves. Then the police advised the townsfolk to go to villages in the east. A party of German SS troops and over one hundred soldiers visited the camp and told us directly, 'Anyone outside after dark will be shot, and artillery will be fired into the camp unless some eight to ten rifles are found and returned.' Later, the Russians said no one was to leave the camp until 'registration' took place. Many of our men slipped away in twos and threes, firmly convinced that they could get through the enemy lines to the Americans. One or two did, but there were many we never saw again.

One day, early in May, two American ambulances pulled in. They loaded up and drove away after telling us that lorries were on the way. Three days later the lorries arrived. They lined up round the wire and said they would be leaving in orderly fashion the next day. However, the Russians were adamant that, under threat of internment, nobody was to board the lorries until they received permission from HQ, and so the prisoners who saw the journey home in sight just stood and watched the trucks drive away.

All this uncertainty was bad for the men. The Senior British Officer had the impossible task, at the request of the Russians, of organising, and indeed been made responsible for, the administration and security of sixteen thousand mixed nationalities. Under such conditions there was a great lowering of spirit and morale of all ranks. When the situation was eased with the arrival of food parcels, allotting the food so

that each man had an equal share became a task. The German ration at this time was half a cup of barley soup and one, two or three boiled potatoes and two slices of black bread per man per day.

Chaos reigned outside as well as inside. Russian troops, with the petty argument that prisoners had to be held until registration had been properly completed, patrolled the area. The remnants of SS divisions were in the woods: there was almost continual gunfire. The citizens in the town began to loot places that were empty. The flour in the bakery disappeared. A very strict curfew was imposed every night and many were shot and hastily buried each day. Days passed, and there was still no sign of American or Russian transport. Many of the men who had completed the long march were still very ill and weak.

I was at the stage where time just stood still. I, who had been so keen in the beginning to escape, realised that the quickest way to return home would have to be by means of an organised withdrawal of prisoners.

I took on the task of quarter-master in a barrack and spent my time measuring loaves of bread so that twenty men received an equal ration of one loaf, and forty men, an equal share of a pound of margarine, and so on, and on and on. Some days, of course, there was nothing to divide except perhaps a cupful of barley to make soup. Cigarettes were scarce and so one or two puffs were enough to quell the pangs of hunger; or so we thought.

A general view of living conditions while waiting for a Russian or American army escort

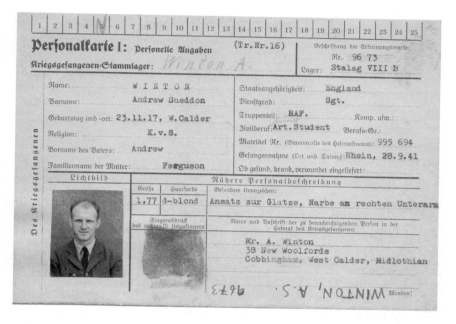

German Identity card

When the guards left the camp, eight of the prisoners took the opportunity to move into their quarters and set about running the RAF personnel from there. This was a very difficult situation as there were French, American, Norwegian, and units from the different War sources in the camp. Going over some cabinets in the Main German Unit, the author found records of all kinds. On one shelf he noticed the name of Winston Churchill and found that he was due to go to the Salt Mines when Germany won the War! Amongst the 'Fleiger' and Escapers, he found his own record – under 'Coal Mines', probably because of his tunnel work! The author promptly removed his card and those of his friends.

Chapter 23

To the Elbe and Home

During the third week in May, when three American ambulances arrived and picked up most of the very sick, we were assured that lorries were on the way. Lorries did arrive, American ones, but again the Russians said, 'No, not until official word came from their HQ', and so the lorries went off empty. It was soul destroying; men turned back to their bunks with tears in their eyes. The Russians promised each day that soon we would be evacuated. Naturally, more doubts as to our destination arose, and then, on the 21st May, a convoy of Russian trucks drove into the camp. We were told that we were to be driven to the Elbe where we would meet Americans.

My kit, such as it was, packed and ready, was put into the seat next to a driver. The back was filled up – no word of registration – and we were off. I looked at the driver.

'Do you speak English?'

He just shook his head and said something to me. I shook my head; that's all that was said all the way to the Elbe. And what a journey!

Roads were lined with destroyed tanks, trucks and other military cars and the remains of firearms. Half-filled graves and dead bodies were strewn at the wood side. Trees were bare and burning, and bodies, swollen in the heat of the sun, lay over trunks. The smell of death and desolation everywhere made me realise that I had been in the midst of a major battlefield.

I got out of the lorry on the eastern bank without even a 'goodbye' to my driver. I set foot on a long pontoon bridge, and walked across to the territory of Americans on the western bank and the first feeling of being free.

First meeting with the Yanks

A long row of American trucks took us on. My driver was a small dark man. When we were ready to move, he took out a very large revolver and loaded it with 'No ole Joe's gonna stop me now,' and we were off on part two of our journey. The scenery gradually improved, and when we reached Halle, we were taken into a hanger with tables set with food. White bread! It tasted like cake. We were given a plate and walked along filling it until we were satisfied. We stayed the night in Halle and after breakfast next day, we went out to the airfield.

I climbed into an old DC10, all rivets and rattling corrugated iron, but good enough to take me to Brussels. One more night there and then out to a beautiful Lancaster. I spoke to the pilot and there was a great coincidence: he was from Forty-Nine Squadron. I spoke gently to him.

'That was my Squadron and I flew out on a Hampden in 1941, so be very careful and get me back safely.'

He called his crew over.

'He flew out from Scampton in '41 in a Hampden!'

They looked me up and down as if I was an antique.

'We'd better get him back – he'll be due some leave now.'

They all shook my hand solemnly and helped me into the plane. A roar from the engines: I was into the air; I was over the sea; I was over green fields; I was back in Guildford. I was back! My long trip was over.

The Lancaster turned slowly, oh so slowly, and drew up beside a very large marquee. A door opened and we were out, and, with knees buckling, we were guided into a tent. There two, white-coated, masked medics grabbed me and a white powder was squirted up both legs; trousers were opened and the self-same powder squirted downwards. Shirtsleeves and neck received the same dose; then I was lifted onto my feet and guided to another tent. Coming towards me, one hand outstretched, a mug of tea in the other, and dressed in a white apron with a red cross, was a lady.

'Come in, laddie. Where do you live? Scotland?'

I nodded.

'Ah weel, we'll soon get you there. Come on.'

I just stood and looked, but I knew that I was smiling with tears in my eyes.

The next week or ten days was a time that I don't really remember. All our clothing was set aside for burning: there was a mad half day to salvage diaries, papers and address books, to have them scrutinised and passed, and then a very special medical examination. Many were directed to special rehabilitation units. A complete new wardrobe was issued and there was interrogation. My story took a long time, but I finally finished my statement and was told I would probably be recalled for details. On to Cosgrove where I received all my ration books, train tickets and leave vouchers, dates to return and three weeks' leave (with the proviso that I could be sent for if necessary) and I was off. Into Waverley between two and three, I walked along Princes Street to the Caley. It was a fine morning and I enjoyed all the noises and smells of bakeries. I was on edge; I wanted to get off at Cobbinshaw and walk home from the morning train. It left on time and half an hour later I steamed out of Harburn.

The loch was quiet – at the far end it was like a mirror with the reflection of the white farmhouse on the top of the hill stretching halfway across – an unforgettable picture. The guard threw out the mailbag and an extra package. The porter gave a receipt, and Jimmy Dewar came to pick them up.

'Hullo, Andrew, you're back! I'm glad to see you. I'm taking this postbag across – you'll get a lift.'

I jumped into his small car and we were away. Mother met me at the door.

'Special delivery this morning, Mrs Winton.'

Before he got into the car, he turned.

'Once you've settled down, come across with your rod. We'll have a day on the loch.'

There was a sort of choking feeling, but I knew that after three years and ten months, I was back to where I had started.

By the KING'S Order the name of
Warrant Officer A.S. Winton,
Royal Air Force Volunteer Reserve,

_ was published in the London Gazette on
13 June, 1946.
as mentioned in a Despatch for distinguished service.
I am charged to record
His Majesty's high appreciation.

Secretary of State for Air

Epilogue

Many incidents on the long march and the closing days of the war have not been recorded in these pages. Images, however, abound: frozen women and children, dead and dying horses, civilians hurrying away from both Germans and Russians, stealing from farms, endless gunfire and planes overhead, dysentery, Percy's sickness and Henry's frostbite, uncertainty, the rush for food, frozen turnips and beet, selling watches for bread, women singing outside a church, the work of Padre Collins, the great spirit of Polish women kicked and jailed and the big-hearted Irish at Stalag 3A.

Woodcut impression of women singing outside a church made on the author's return to Art College

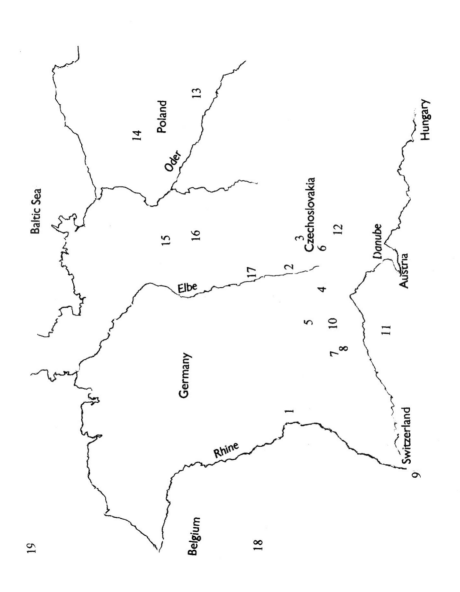

Key to Map

1. Dulag Luft to Lamsdorf
2. Lamsdorf Stalag 8B to Neutischen
3. Neutischen to Brno
4. Brno to Buchenwald
5. Buchenwald to Brno
6. Brno to Zlin
7. Zlin to Lamsdorf and Hohenfels Stalag 383
8. Hohenfels to Switzerland
9. Switzerland to Hohenfels
10. Hohenfels to Munich
11. Munich to Hohenfels
12. Hohenfels to Bankau and onto unidentified village in Poland
13. Unidentified village to Warsaw
14. Warsaw to Berlin
15. Berlin to Luckenwelde
16. Luckenwelde to Halle
17. Halle to Brussels
18. Brussels to England
19. To Scotland

Books from Cualann Press

Beyond the Bamboo Screen
Scottish Prisoners of War under the Japanese
Extracts from Newsletters of the Scottish Far East Prisoner of War Association
and Other Sources
Tom McGowran OBE
Illustrations by G S Gimson QC

ISBN 0 9535036 1 5

Price £9.99

On Flows the Tay
Perth and the First World War
Dr Bill Harding Ph.D., FEIS

ISBN 0 9535036 2 3

Price £12.99

Under the Shadow
Letters of Love and War
The Poignant Testimony and Story of Hugh Wallace Mann and Jessie Reid
Narrative: Bríd Hetherington

ISBN 0 9535036 0 7

Price £12.99

Of Fish and Men
Tales of a Scottish Fisher
David C Watson

ISBN 09535036 3 1

Price £10.99

New Titles from Cualann Press

The Lion and the Eagle

Reminiscences of Polish Veterans in Scotland during the Second World War

Editor: Dr Diana M Henderson LLB TD FSA Scot

Foreword: His Excellency Dr Stanislaw Komorowski, Ambassador of the Republic of Poland at the Court of St James

ISBN: 0 9535036 4 X **£9.99**

Stand By Your Beds!

A Wry Look at National Service

David Findlay Clark OBE, MA, Ph.D., C.Psychol., F.B.Ps.S.

Preface: Trevor Royle

ISBN: 0 9535036 6 6 **£13.99**